An Hachette UK Company
www.hachette.co.uk

First published in the United Kingdom in 2020 by
Ilex, an imprint of
Octopus Publishing Group Ltd
Carmelite House
50 Victoria Embankment
London EC4Y 0DZ
www.octopusbooks.co.uk

Publisher: Alison Starling
Editorial Director: Zena Alkayat
Managing Editor: Rachel Silverlight
Editor: Jenny Dye
Editorial Assistant: Ellen Sandford O'Neill
Art Director: Ben Gardiner
Designer: Studio Polka
Photographer: Kim Lightbody
Illustrator: Caitlin Keegan
Stylist: Rachel Vere
Production Manager: Caroline Alberti

ISBN 978-1-78157-758-5

A CIP catalogue record for this book is available
from the British Library.

Printed and bound in China

10 9 8

YOU WILL BE ABLE TO CROCHET BY THE END OF THIS BOOK

ZOE BATEMAN

ilex

Introduction

Stitch and Technique Library

Projects

Introduction

First of all, welcome! If this is the beginning of your crochet journey, I can promise you that once you get going, you'll be completely hooked (yes, that is a crochet-related pun!).

I can still remember picking up a hook for the first time – I couldn't hold my yarn comfortably and my stitches were like knots, so I understand it can be daunting. But with good guidance and just a little bit of practice on a regular basis, you'll be amazed by how quickly you will improve. You might find it tricky at first, and those initial practise stitches you make will be all kinds of wonky, but very soon it will become more relaxing and rewarding.

This book has been designed to make it easy to look up any topic. There is a whole section on stitches and techniques for you to master before you're let loose on the projects. All the projects have been chosen for their simplicity – they are straightforward, with no fuss or frills, while still being beautiful and practical. The patterns gradually increase in skill level, but they are all suitable for beginners.

For me, crochet is part of my self-care routine, and I usually crochet for at least half an hour before bed as I find it a great way to practise mindfulness. The repetition of stitches and the motion of wrapping the yarn round the hook all help to take you into a state where your worries seem to lessen.

Crochet is also incredibly rewarding. Turning a ball of yarn into a blanket, a toy or an item of clothing, using just a hook and your hands, is almost like magic. My aim is to introduce as many people as possible to this craft, and to show you that it does not have to be complicated and that anyone can learn to crochet.

How to use this book

The way you use this book will depend on your skills. If you are a total beginner and have never picked up a hook before, then I recommend starting at the beginning of the book and working through it stage by stage. Start by learning about yarn and hooks, move on to practising your chains and then try out some of the basic stitches, before moving on to the first project.

The projects in this book are designed to build up your knowledge progressively, giving you time to practise and master each skill before moving on to the next level. So, if this is your first time crocheting, it's best not to jump straight in with the penguin toy (see page 146). I totally understand why you would want to – he is very cute and cuddly – but if you start off with the ear warmer (see page 88), you'll be able to build up your skills gradually. You'll learn to read a pattern, change yarn colour, increase and decrease stitches and more, growing in confidence with each project you take on.

If you are already able to crochet, you can use this book to try out a new technique that you might not know – perhaps you've only worked in rows and want to have a go at crocheting rounds. Choose a project that suits you, and get stuck in. There are helpful hints along the way to make it easier.

Alternatively, if you're feeling like expanding your crochet horizons, you can use this book as a jumping-off point and try adapting some of the patterns. They are designed to be simple enough for beginners, but that makes them ideal for customizing and adding your own flair to, once you feel confident enough. Perhaps you'll turn the wall hanging (see page 124) into a cushion or use the colour block squares (see page 100) to make a jumper. One of the many reasons I love crochet so much is its adaptability, so if you're a more advanced crocheter I hope this book encourages you to experiment.

'Crochet is incredibly
rewarding. Turning
a ball of yarn into a
blanket, a toy or an item
of clothing, using just
a hook and your hands,
is almost like magic.'

Yarn

When you first start crocheting, the choice of yarns available on the market may appear daunting, but once you understand the technical terms such as 'weight' and 'fibre' you'll be able to select yarns for your projects like a pro.

YARN WEIGHT

The term 'yarn weight' doesn't refer to the actual weight of the ball or 'skein', but rather to the thickness of the yarn strand. There is a name for each weight and these vary between the UK and the US, so below is a table with the equivalent terms.

Yarns can vary from being as thin as embroidery thread, right up to Super Chunky. There will be some variation within a particular yarn weight – not all Chunky yarns are of equal thickness – so pay attention when mixing different brands of yarn in the same project.

UK	US
4-ply	Sport
DK (Double Knit)	DK or Light Worsted
Aran	Worsted
Chunky	Bulky
Super Chunky	Super Bulky

YARN FIBRE

An important consideration when choosing your yarn is the fibre or fibre mix. There is a huge range on the market and the chart below lists some of the common ones. Personally, I prefer blends of natural and synthetic fibres, such as wool and acrylic. These combine the best properties of each fibre to create a yarn that is durable, but also soft.

	PROS	CONS
ACRYLIC	+ Widely available and economically priced + Comes in a huge range of colours to suit any palette + Very hard-wearing and easily machine-washable	+ Can feel rough or scratchy against the skin
COTTON	+ A natural material which feels soft against the skin + Lightweight, so ideal for spring/summer projects + Hard-wearing + Widely available in an excellent range of colours + Smooth finish makes it ideal for toys	+ Does not often come in heavier yarn weights + The fibres can split and be difficult to work with + Cannot be washed at high temperatures due to risk of shrinkage
WOOL	+ Can be incredibly soft and feels lovely against the skin + Natural material, so breathable	+ More expensive than acrylic and cotton + Not as hard-wearing and at risk of moths + Must be hand washed carefully
MOHAIR AND ALPACA	+ Incredibly soft with a beautiful finish + Produces lovely textural effects in finished pieces + Feels lovely against the skin	+ Can be extremely pricey + Colour ranges and yarn weights are usually very limited + Delicate, so must be looked after very carefully

READING YOUR YARN BAND

When choosing yarn in a shop, check the information on the yarn band (that strip of paper wrapped round the ball) carefully to make sure you've got the correct one for your project. When you buy online, this information will be included in the listing. Every brand has different yarn bands, but they will usually include:

Brand name
The name of the manufacturer or spinner.

Yarn name
The name of the individual yarn type.

Yarn weight
For example, 'DK', 'Aran' or 'Chunky'.

Fibre or fibre mix
For example, '50% cotton/50% acrylic'.

Colour
Usually a reference number, but may also have a name, such as 0136 Buttercup Yellow.

Dye lot
The number assigned to the dye batch for that particular ball. If you are making an item that uses multiple balls of the same colour, make sure they are all from the same dye lot to avoid any slight variations in colour.

Ball weight
Given in grams in the UK. Most balls will be either 50g or 100g.

Yarn length
Given in metres. It's important to check how much yarn you need for a project against how much is in a ball – a 100g ball of one type may contain 80m, but in another yarn it may contain 60m.

Recommended hook size
The ideal hook to use with the yarn.

WHICH YARN TO USE

When you begin any new project, your choice of yarn will depend on what you are making as well as the effect you want to achieve. If you are following a pattern it will usually recommend a yarn, but you might not always want to use the same one. When choosing or substituting a yarn the most important things to consider are:

Yarn weight
You could make a cushion using any weight, but your end result will look completely different if you use DK compared to Super Chunky. Also, it's worth remembering that the heavier the weight, the thicker the yarn, and so the more quickly your project will work up. If you are using a pattern and are swapping yarns, you will need the same yarn weight as used in the pattern.

Fibre
Consider the size of your project, the amount of yarn required and how much it will cost – acrylic and cotton are more economical than pure wool. Also think about whether the item will be worn against the skin and how frequently it will need to be washed. If it will be subjected to a lot of wear and tear, remember that synthetic and cotton yarns are easy to care for.

Colour
Use any colour you like – this is where you have the most freedom. Your colour choice will not affect the technical aspects of the pattern, but you should consider its practicality, as well as how it will fit with your decor or wardrobe.

Length
Always check the length per ball of the suggested yarn and ensure you match this when substituting. If the recommended yarn has 100m per ball and uses three balls, you need 300m of your alternative. So, if your substitute yarn only has 80m per ball you will need to order four balls.

Hooks

I am going to talk you through some of the different hooks available and which yarns to use with them. Your choice of hook is mostly down to personal preference, so the key is to try out a few different types and see which one you like best. If you are finding a particular hook uncomfortable to hold or tricky to crochet with, then try a different type.

HOOK TYPES

Wooden hooks
These can be made from either wood or lightweight bamboo. They have a smooth sanded or varnished finish to prevent any splinters which could snag the yarn.

Plastic hooks
Made from solid plastic, these are smooth to use, but beware of buying super-cheap versions as they may have ridges where the yarn can get caught.

Metal hooks
Hooks for very fine yarn are called thread hooks and are made from steel to prevent them from bending while you crochet. Larger hooks are usually aluminium to keep them lightweight.

Ergonomic hooks
These have a more comfortable grip, and are ideal when you're crocheting for long periods of time, or if you have a condition such as carpal tunnel syndrome or repetitive strain injury. The metal shaft of the hook is set into a larger handle made from dense foam or rubber.

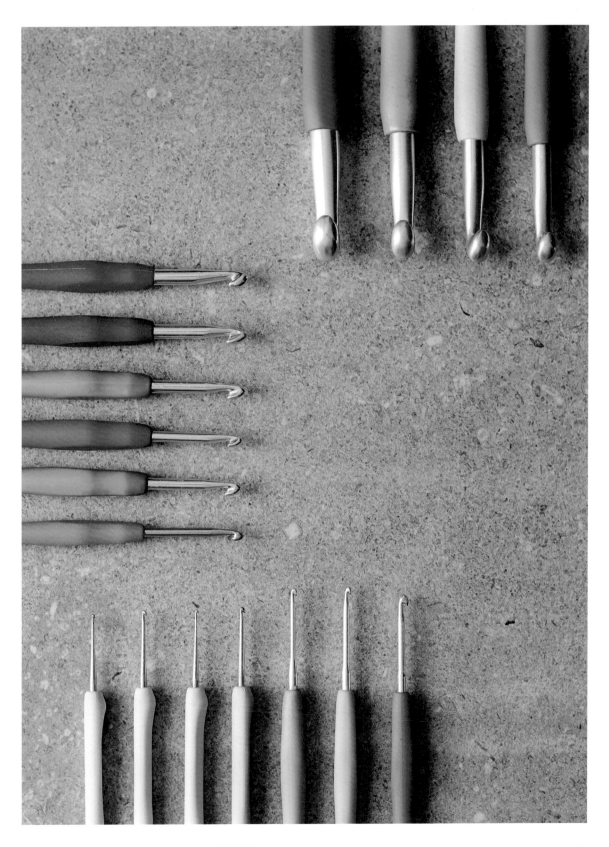

HOOK SIZES

As with yarn weight, the UK and US have different ways of identifying crochet hook sizes. The UK uses the metric system which gives a measurement in millimetres (mm). This represents the diameter of your crochet hook at the widest point (the widest point of the actual hook – not of the handle).

If you are working from a US pattern the hook size will often be given as a letter with a number. This handy conversion chart will help you figure out which hook to choose if you are using a US pattern but have hooks labelled in millimetres or vice versa. The chart also includes the old UK sizes. If you have a vintage crochet hook, perhaps inherited from a family member, it may be marked with one of these numbers.

METRIC	US	OLD UK
2.00 mm	B/1	14
2.25 mm		13
2.50 mm	C/2	12
3.00 mm		11
3.25 mm	D/3	10
3.50 mm	E/4	9
3.75 mm	F/5	
4.00 mm	G/6	8
4.25 mm		
4.50 mm	7	7
5.00 mm	H/8	6
5.50 mm	I/9	5
6.00 mm	J/10	4
6.50 mm	K/10.5	3
7.00 mm		2
8.00 mm	L/11	0
9.00 mm	M/13	00
10.00 mm	N/15	000
12.00 mm	O/16	
15.00 mm	P/19	
16.00 mm	Q	
17.50 mm	R	
19.00 mm	S/35	

WHICH HOOK TO USE FOR YOUR YARN

The yarn band will usually tell you the most suitable hook size for that particular yarn, but I have included this useful chart in case you've taken the yarn band off (and lost it). It shows some of the most popular yarn weights and their recommended hooks. It's important to remember that these are only meant as a guideline – there are plenty of times when you may choose to use a different size hook, for example:

To achieve the correct tension
Tension is explained on page 69. If you are following a pattern where the finished dimensions of your crochet need to be precise, you may need to use a bigger or smaller hook to achieve the recommended tension and therefore the correct size.

When making amigurumi toys
Because crochet toys will be stuffed, it's important that the fabric is very tight to avoid any of the filling poking out. Unless you naturally work with a very tight tension you will usually go down a full hook size to help you to crochet more tightly than normal.

If you want to achieve a particular effect
By changing the recommended hook size you can create a fabric with a completely different look. This is usually done with a larger hook. For example, I crocheted myself a snood with a Super Chunky yarn and the suggested hook size was 10mm. I used a 15mm hook instead and it made the snood much looser and more open.

UK NAME	US NAME	HOOK SIZE (MM)
2-ply	Lace-weight	0.75mm–1.5mm
3-ply	Sock/Fingering	2mm–2.5mm
4-ply	Sport	3mm
Double Knit (DK)	DK or Light Worsted	4mm
Aran	Worsted	5mm
Chunky	Bulky	6mm–8mm
Super Chunky	Super Bulky	8mm plus

Other tools and equipment

One of the great things about crochet is that you don't need lots of fancy tools – all you really need is a hook and yarn. There are, however, a few extra tools that come in handy.

Tape measure or ruler

A measuring tool will come in handy when you are making sample swatches and need to check your tension (see page 69), as well as for making an item of a specific size, such as a cushion cover to fit a pad.

Stitch markers

These are small plastic or metal clasps that fasten on to the stitch you want to mark and you can pick up packs relatively cheaply. They are mostly used when working in rounds. But I also use one to hold my working loop when I'm partway through a project, so that it doesn't unravel while it's inside my bag. I also use a stitch marker to help me keep track of how many chains I've done when starting a new project. A small scrap of yarn will work fine as an alternative, but I find stitch markers quicker and easier to use (and less likely to get lost!).

Yarn needles

These are longer and thicker than sewing needles, with a blunt tip and a large eye for threading yarn. They are used for weaving in yarn ends (see page 78) at the end of a project and also when sewing crocheted pieces together. An item worked in single crochet with a DK yarn will require a smaller needle than one worked in Super Chunky yarn.

Pompom makers

You can make pompoms the old-fashioned way using two cardboard circles, but these plastic versions are reusable and super fast to use. They make perfect fluffy pompoms every time.

Project bag

I keep each project in its own bag with the correct yarn, a copy of the pattern and the correct hook. This means it's always easy to pick up and work on a project, as everything is together. It also makes it easy for me to see if I have enough yarn for a project as it's all right there.

Hook organizer

Before I purchased my hook organizer, I would spend hours hunting for the right hook. Now all of my hooks are together in one place, organized neatly by size, ready to go.

Crochet journals

Using a journal allows you to keep track of what you have created, note down information about the pieces you are currently working on, and plan your future projects. Crochet journals can take many forms, such as a notebook, a digital file, or a note-keeping app. The format is up to you – personally, I use a combination of a mini folder with inserts and a crochet projects board on the Trello app. In this section I am going to focus on what you can record in your own journal, as well as some tips I've learned over the years of keeping mine.

WHY SHOULD YOU KEEP A CROCHET JOURNAL?

Tracking your crochet projects means you can recreate any of them. It's also handy when someone asks about the yarn you used for a particular project.

A journal is also helpful when you are planning what to make next. I always have enough yarn in my stash for around five to ten future projects, and when I place the order I always write down which project it's for. This means I don't accidentally use the yarn for another project and also helps prevent me going on a 'yarn spree' where I purchase random yarns that I don't need!

So, what should you record in your journal? For both completed projects and works in progress, always write down as much detail as possible. Here is what I include for each of my projects:

<u>Where I found the pattern</u>
If it's an online pattern I write down the URL as well as the creator's social media handles, so I can credit them if I share the finished item. If it's from a book I write down the title, author, ISBN number and the page number of the pattern.

A copy of the pattern
Patterns sometimes get removed from the internet or the user changes their URL, and books get mislaid or lent to another crocheter. Having your own printed copy means you don't have to spend hours hunting for the pattern.

The yarn used
Write down the brand and name, as well as the shade and dye lot. I also keep a note of how much yarn the project required, both in number of balls and length, for example '3.5 balls, approx. 365m'. This is also where you can record any notes about the yarn itself – whether it is particularly nice to work with, or if it tends to be 'splitty'. This helps you to know whether or not to use the same yarn again.

Yarn swatch
It can be hard to remember exactly what a yarn was like just from the information on the yarn band, so I always tie a few strands of each yarn I use onto a paper tag.

The hook used
Make a note of which size hook or hooks you use for each project. Also write down whether this was the size recommended in the pattern so you know whether your tension was too loose or too tight.

Notes on the pattern
This is probably one of the best reasons for keeping a crochet journal. When I'm crocheting from someone else's pattern I will often make changes, which might be as simple as working a few extra rows on a blanket or adding a decorative border. If you don't keep a record of these changes, then chances are you won't remember exactly what you did if you try to recreate the project at a later date. It's also a great chance to write a mini review of the pattern: how difficult it was, how long it took and anything to serve as a reminder if you decide to make it again.

INTRODUCTION

PLANNING FUTURE PROJECTS

For projects that you'd like to make in the future, write down information or ideas as soon as you get them, so when you are ready to start crocheting you're not racking your brains trying to remember where you saw that amazing jumper pattern. In addition to where you found the pattern and a hard copy, it's a good idea to make a few extra notes and use the journal wisely.

<u>Why you want to crochet this project</u>
This may sound a bit strange, but trust me, several times I've bought yarn for patterns and then could not remember why I had decided to make it. If it's a present for friends or family (such as a new baby gift), write down the date you'd like to give it to them by. If it's for yourself, write down your vision for the project, which could be something like 'blanket to go on bed in guest room – crochet in shades of purple with a pompom border.'

<u>Which yarn to use</u>
If you have a particular yarn in mind, write down all the details as well as whether or not you have already purchased it.

<u>Project inspiration</u>
Sometimes you might get an idea for a crochet project but haven't found a specific pattern. Collect images of anything that inspires you – these don't necessarily have to be actual crochet items, but could be photos that have a colour scheme or a texture that you'd like to use. For example, if I wanted to make a cute baby outfit for a friend's newborn, I would gather some inspirational images of the sort of thing I want to make, to help me refine my thoughts.

<u>Keep it fun</u>
Remember, a crochet journal is meant to help you remember what you have made in the past and plan your future makes. It should be a fun process and shouldn't take up too much of your time, so don't agonise over it. Do, however, spend time making it visually appealing, whether that's keeping it very simple and minimal, or decorating it with stickers and cuttings.

Stitch and

Technique Library

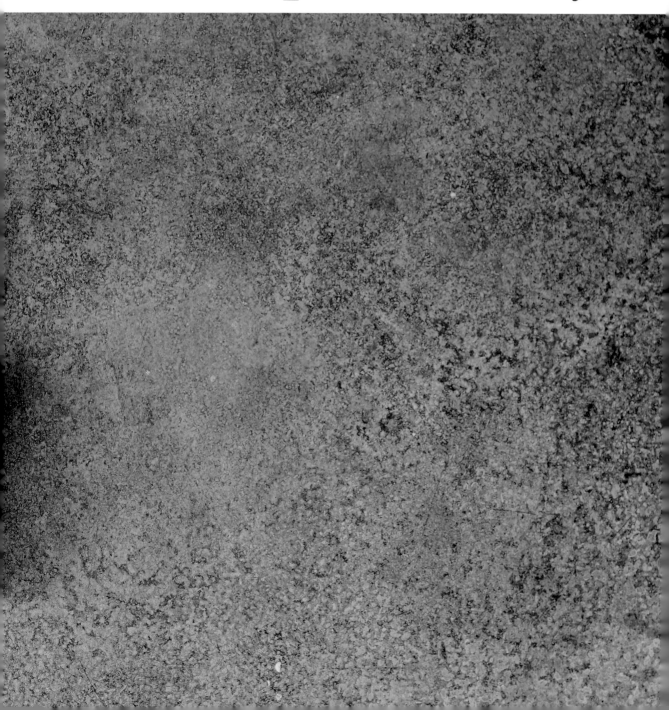

US vs UK terminology

The UK and US have different names for most of the crochet stitches. Although I am a UK crocheter, I have used US crochet terms throughout this book. The reason for this (and why I teach all my crochet students the US system) is that the vast majority of patterns I find online and in books and magazines are written with US crochet terms, so it makes sense to learn them and then have the option to convert to UK terms as needed. Below is a handy table for converting from US to UK crochet terms. Just remember to double-check which system your pattern is using before you start, otherwise you may end up having to undo a lot of work!

US CROCHET TERMS	UK CROCHET TERMS
Chain stitch	Chain stitch
Slipstitch	Slipstitch
Single crochet	Double crochet
Half-double crochet	Half-treble crochet
Double crochet	Treble crochet
Treble crochet	Double treble crochet
Double treble crochet	Triple treble crochet

Reading patterns

Pattern reading is definitely a skill and, particularly when you are a beginner, you may find yourself longing for more detailed instructions. This is why I have added extra notes to help explain the stages and techniques in my patterns. The more patterns you read, the easier it will get, so stick with it.

ABBREVIATIONS

When you look at a crochet pattern, you will see that the stitch names are abbreviated rather than written out in full. This is to save time, save space on the page and to make it easier to follow the instructions. So, rather than a pattern saying 'crochet four chain stitches, then crochet four double crochets', it will simply say 'ch4, 4dc'. This chart gives the abbreviation for each stitch.

You don't need to memorize hundreds of different stitches – as long as you know the abbreviations for the basic crochet stitches you will be fine. Make sure you check whether the pattern uses the US or UK crochet terms.

STITCH NAME	ABBREVIATION
Chain stitch	ch
Slipstitch	slst
Single crochet	sc
Half-double crochet	hdc
Half-treble crochet	htr
Double crochet	dc
Treble crochet	tr
Double treble crochet	dtr
Triple treble crochet	ttr

TAIL END AND WORKING YARN

The working yarn is the yarn attached to the ball, and the tail end is the cut end of yarn.

YARN OVER

This is written as 'yo' and means to bring the working yarn over the back of the hook.

REPEATS

Rows or rounds that are repeated are indicated by the numbers at the beginning of each line.

> 'Row 5–14: dc in each st.'

Here you have to repeat the same instruction (double crochet in each stitch) for Row 5, Row 6 and so on, up to and including Row 14.

ASTERISKS

These are used to indicate instructions that are to be repeated. Anything before the asterisk is not repeated.

> 'Row 7: Ch3, dc in first st. *2dc in st, sc in next st.
> Repeat from * to end.'

This means repeat '2dc in st, sc in next st' all the way along the row, but not the 'Ch3, dc in first st' at the beginning.

STITCH NUMBERS

Numbers in brackets at the end of a row or round show how many stitches you should have. These aren't always given, especially if there isn't much increasing or decreasing. But when you see them, count your stitches to check you are following the instructions correctly.

> 'Round 5: *Dc, inc. *Repeat around (18).'

Here you should have 18 stitches in total when you reach the end of Round 5.

SUBHEADINGS

Pay attention to subheadings within patterns, as these indicate which part of the pattern you are working on. This is particularly important for items such as toys or clothing that are made in several sections and then joined together.

Right-handed vs left-handed crochet

Even though most tutorials show a hook being held in the right hand, learning to crochet when you're left-handed is not a daunting prospect. In fact, it's very similar to crocheting right-handed, with just a few exceptions, which I've outlined below. Aside from these points, the technique is the same for all crocheters. You will still bring the yarn over the hook towards you, still turn your hook towards you and still insert your hook from the front to the back. The only difference is that you will be holding the hook in your left hand instead of your right.

Holding the hook
Some left-handed people prefer to hold their hook in their right hand, but most will use their dominant left hand to hold the hook, with their right hand controlling the yarn – the opposite way round to right-handed crocheters.

Direction
You will need to crochet from left to right when working in rows, instead of from right to left. When working in rounds, you will crochet clockwise instead of anti-clockwise.

Reading patterns
When working from a pattern, you should read each line of instructions from end to start, as you will start a row where a right-handed crocheter would be finishing. Usually you won't need to worry about this, as the pattern will be the same in both directions. For patterns such as garments that involve shaping, you will need to start at the end of the instructions for a particular row or round, and work backwards.

Holding your hook

When you first pick up a crochet hook it will feel awkward in your hand, and you may struggle to control it. Don't panic – this is totally normal. Part of getting into the swing of things quickly is finding a way to hold your hook that works for you. As long as you feel comfortable and you're able to manoeuvre the hook easily, then you're doing great. Try out the three different holds below while you chain stitch, to see which works best for you.

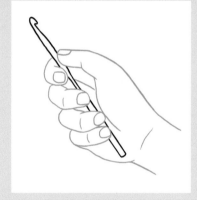

THE PENCIL GRIP
Hold the hook exactly as you would a pen or pencil, with the handle outside your hand.

THE KNIFE GRIP
Grasp the hook as if you are holding a knife and are about to cut up your dinner. The handle should be tucked inside your hand.

THE OVERHAND GRIP
Hold the hook in your fist with your fingers curled around the handle.

Holding your yarn

The way you hold your yarn controls the tension of your work, so finding the best way to do this is crucial to successful crochet. The aim is to make all your stitches the same size by keeping the tension (also known as the 'gauge') consistent (see page 69). Your non-dominant hand controls the flow of yarn to your hook. The more yarn it lets through, the looser your stitches. The less yarn it lets through, the tighter they are. A regular tension will give you perfectly neat rows and stitches, so it's good to practise!

There isn't really a right or wrong way to hold your yarn – every crocheter holds it differently. So find what's comfortable for you.

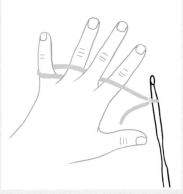

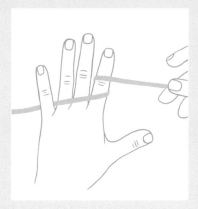

THE LITTLE FINGER METHOD
Wrap the yarn around your little finger, from right to left, then carry it across the back of your other fingers. Raise your index finger to create tension on the yarn.

THE LITTLE FINGER METHOD ADAPTATION
If the method doesn't feel comfortable, try passing the yarn under your middle finger as shown. You will still need to raise your index finger to create tension, but this method can help to give you more control.

THE INDEX FINGER METHOD
Start with the yarn under your little finger, then carry it across the next three fingers before wrapping it back around the index finger, from right to left. Raise your middle finger to control the tension.

Tying a slip knot

Tying a slip knot is the first thing you will do when starting to crochet. It attaches your yarn to your hook so that you are ready to make a stitch.

1.
Make a loop with your yarn from left to right, making sure the working yarn (the yarn attached to the ball) is on top and the tail end (the cut end) is underneath.

2.
Insert your hook into the loop and use it to grab the working yarn. Pull the yarn back through the loop.

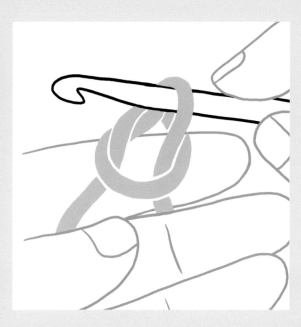
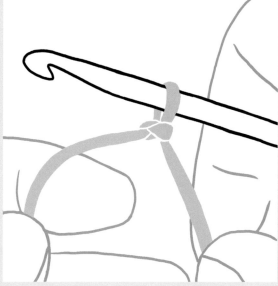

3.
Pull the tail end of yarn and the working yarn downwards at the same time to neaten up your slip knot. You will have a loop around the hook, with the knot underneath.

4.
To tighten up the knot, simply pull the working yarn and the tail end apart. This will make the loop on your hook smaller. Don't pull it too tight as you will struggle to crochet, but make sure it's not so loose that it falls off your hook.

Chain stitch (ch)

Chain stitch may be the simplest of all crochet stitches and it is used to make the first row – the 'foundation chain' – of many projects. The name is abbreviated to 'ch' in patterns, often followed by a number, so 'ch2' means two chain stitches and 'ch3' means three chain stitches, and so on.

 Practise making chain stitches until the movements feel natural and all your stitches are the same size.

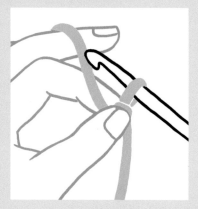 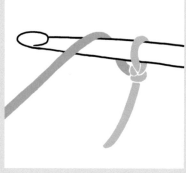

1.
Start by joining the yarn to your hook with a slip knot (see page 32). Hold your yarn and hook in whichever way feels most comfortable to you.

 Use your thumb and index (or middle) finger of your non-dominant hand to pinch the yarn just below the slip knot to keep your first loop steady.

2.
Bring your yarn over the crochet hook, from the back to the front. This is called 'yarn over' and is written in patterns as 'yo.'

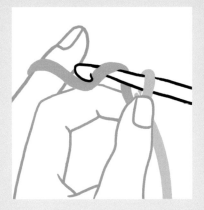

3.
Keeping tension on your yarn, slide your crochet hook back until the 'yarn over' is sitting in the curve of your hook. Make sure the hook is turned towards you so that the curve is facing down towards the base of the loop. If your yarn keeps slipping out from your hook, it usually means you don't have enough tension.

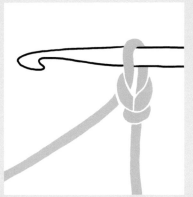

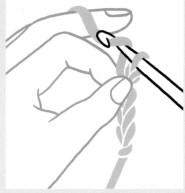

4.
Draw the 'yarn over' through the loop on your hook (the slip knot), being careful to stop once you've pulled it through. If you keep going the loop is likely to come off the end of the hook. You've now made your first chain stitch.

If you're finding it hard to get the hook through the loop this may be because you either haven't got your hook turned all the way down, or because your loop is too tight. To loosen the loop, pull upwards with the hook and relax the tension slightly.

5.
Repeat the previous steps to crochet as many chain stitches as your pattern requires. As the row grows, keep moving your thumb and index finger upwards so they are always pinching quite close to your hook. This will help you to stabilize and control your work.

Counting chain stitches

Learning how to count your stitches is an essential part of learning to crochet, particularly the stitches in your foundation chain. As with everything else, the more you do it, the easier it becomes. If you start with the wrong number it can throw off the whole pattern, so I'll show you how to identify and count your chains.

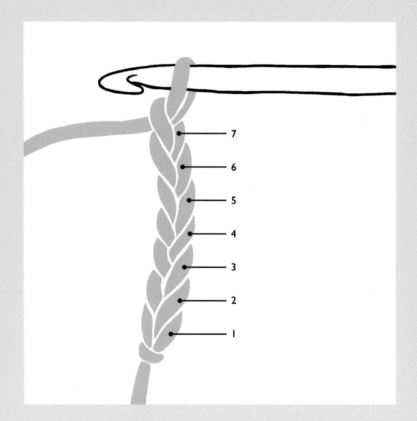

Chain stitches have a front and a back. The front looks smooth and has a 'V'-shaped, braided look to it. You count each 'V' as one stitch.

Do note: whether you're counting from the front or the back, the loop on your hook doesn't count as a stitch. If you are crocheting a long foundation chain – perhaps you're beginning a project like a large blanket – it is useful to place a stitch marker (see page 18) every 20 stitches or so. This means that if you lose count you don't have to start again from the beginning.

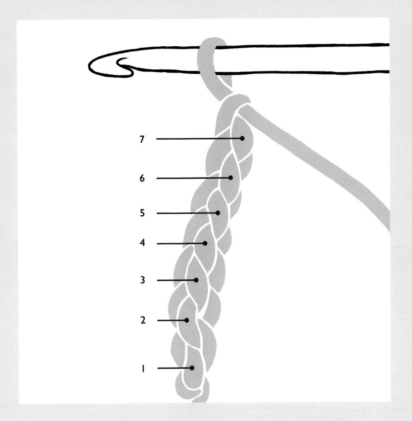

The back has a sort of bump between each stitch and it is these bumps that you count. It doesn't matter which side you count from, so try both and choose whichever you find easiest.

Where to insert your hook

If you are a newbie to crochet, it's normal to feel unsure about where to insert your hook when you're working into a stitch. As with most skills, the more you do it the easier it will get. This is useful information to refer to when mastering the stitches on the following pages.

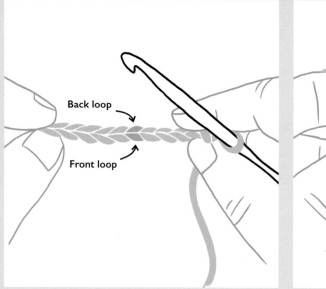

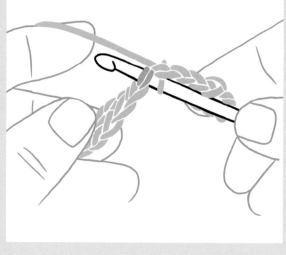

1.
Start by looking at the top of a row of stitches, from a bird's-eye view, so that you can see the 'V' shapes. There are two pieces of yarn that form each 'V'. These are referred to as the 'front loop' (the one near to you) and the 'back loop' (the one that's further away).

2a.
<u>Working under both loops</u>
You will usually insert your hook under both the front and back loops so, unless your pattern tells you otherwise, always assume you need to go under the 'V'.

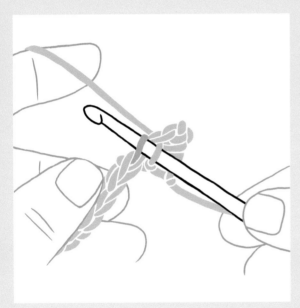

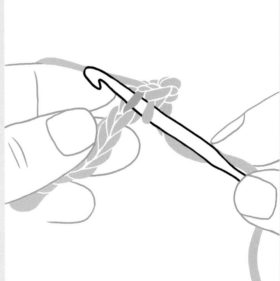

2b.

<u>Working in the back loop</u>

Some patterns may ask you to work in the 'BLO', which stands for 'back loop only'. This means that instead of putting your hook under both loops, you slide it under just the back loop. The ribbed pompom hat and scarf patterns (see pages 94 and 98) are worked using this technique, which produces a lovely textured effect.

2c.

<u>Working in the front loop</u>

Alternatively, a pattern may ask you to work in the 'FLO', which stands for 'front loop only'. This means that you insert your hook under the loop that is nearer to you. Combining BLO and FLO in stitches such as Waffle Stitch (see page 72) gives an extra dimension to your crochet.

Working in a stitch vs a space

The type of stitch you are working into determines where you insert your hook to make a new stitch.

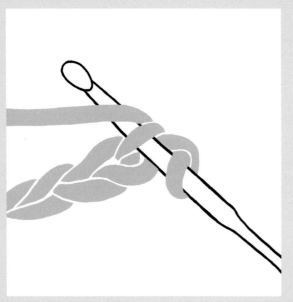

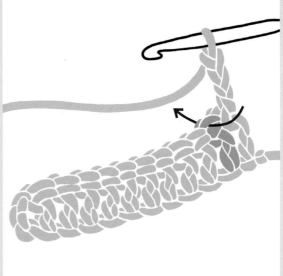

CHAIN STITCH

When working into a chain stitch, insert your hook through the centre of the stitch when looking at it from the front. One side of the stitch will end up above the hook, and the other will be underneath the hook.

WORKING INTO OTHER STITCHES

If you are crocheting into a single, half-double, double or treble, insert your hook underneath the two loops that make up the top 'V'-shaped part of the stitch, ensuring it goes into the actual stitch rather than into the space between two stitches.

WORKING INTO A SPACE

Spaces in a crochet pattern are usually created by working chain stitches and skipping over stitches in the row below to make a gap in the work. Work your stitches for the next row into these open spaces instead of into the chain stitches. Simply insert your hook under the chain and through the space, then complete the stitch as normal. Sometimes your pattern will specifically state this:

'5dc into 3ch space'

This means you work five double crochet stitches into the space that was created when you chained three stitches on the previous row. But it may not always specify that you can work into the space – if it doesn't, just assume you can do so anyway. It will save you a lot of time and frustration, and save you from trying to insert your hook into fiddly chain stitches.

Turning your work

As you learn the stitches in the following pages, you'll find you will create rows of stitches. When you are working in a row, you will eventually reach the end and run out of stitches to crochet into. At this point, you will need to turn your work so that you can crochet back into the stitches you have just made.

1.
Turn your work clockwise, so you are bringing the stitches you have just completed round towards you and then keep turning so they extend out to the left.

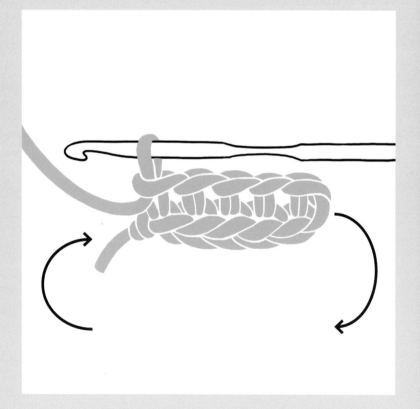

2.
Your hook should now be on the
right and the stitches on the left.
You can now start crocheting the
next row.

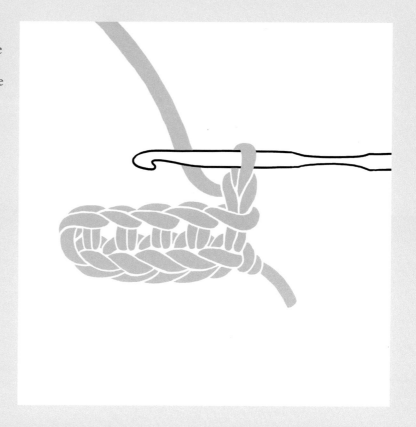

Single crochet (sc)

Single crochet is the shortest basic crochet stitch and it creates the most tightly woven fabric. It is used in most amigurumi and toy patterns because the dense texture means that the stuffing can't escape. But it has lots of other uses too – I have used it in my plant pot cover (see page 128) and storage basket (see page 134) patterns to create pieces that will stand up on their own.

Step 1 of a single crochet will vary depending on whether it is your first or a subsequent row.

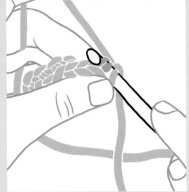

1a.
Work your first row of single crochet into your foundation chain (see page 34). Skip the first chain stitch (the one nearest the hook) and insert your hook into the second stitch along.

1b.
If you are starting a subsequent row and working into existing stitches, start by making one chain stitch (your turning chain, see page 54). Insert your hook under both loops (the 'V') of the first stitch in the previous row.

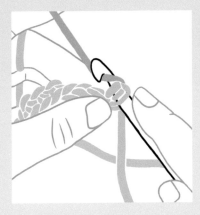

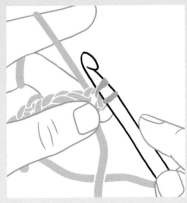

2.
Bring your yarn over your hook from right to left, as you would when making a chain stitch.

3.
Pull the yarn through the first two loops on your hook (the 'V' of the stitch that you inserted your hook into). You now have two loops on your hook.

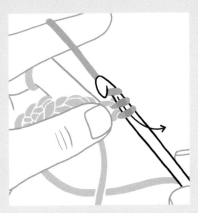

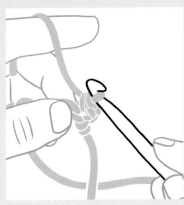

4.
Bring the yarn over your hook again from right to left. Then draw the hook through both loops, pulling your yarn with it. If you are struggling to do this, try slightly relaxing your tension on the working yarn and angle your hook upwards to loosen the loops.

5.
You have now completed a single crochet stitch. To make the next one, insert your hook into the next stitch along and begin again.

Half-double crochet (hdc)

As with single crochet, the first step of working a half-double crochet will vary depending on whether it is your first row (you are working into your foundation chain) or a subsequent row (you are working into a previous row of stitches).

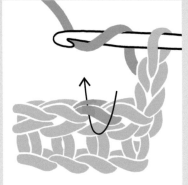

1a.
To crochet your first row of half-double crochet, start by working into your foundation chain.

Skip the first two chain stitches (counting from the one nearest to your hook) and bring your yarn over your hook. Insert your hook into the third stitch from the hook as shown.

1b.
However, if you are starting a subsequent row you will chain two to start – these will become your turning chains or a 'fake' half-double crochet (hdc).

Because these chains count as the first stitch on your new row, you will skip the first stitch, bring the yarn over the hook, and insert the hook under both loops of the second stitch from the previous row.

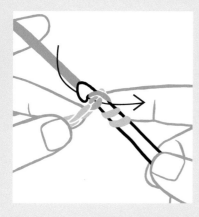 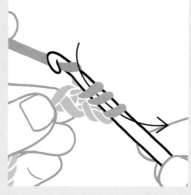 

2.
Bring your yarn over your hook again, and pull through the stitch (the first two loops) on your hook.

3.
You now have three loops on your hook. Bring your yarn over your hook once more, and pull it through these three loops. You don't have to pull through them all in one go, so take your time.

Be careful not to snag your hook as you pull it through the loops as this can mean you pull an extra loop through with you.

4.
You should now have one loop left on your hook. This means you've successfully completed a half-double crochet.

Double crochet (dc)

As with the other crochet stitches, the first step of working a double crochet will vary depending on whether it is your first row (you are working into your foundation chain) or a subsequent row (you are working into a previous row of stitches).

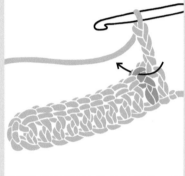

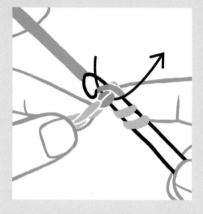

1a.
To crochet your first row of double crochet you will first work into your foundation chain.

Skip the first three chain stitches (counting from the one nearest to the hook) and bring your yarn over your hook. Insert your hook into the fourth stitch from the hook as shown. You are skipping more chain stitches than with a half-double stitch, as double crochet is slightly taller.

1b.
However, if you are starting a subsequent row you need to chain three to start – these will become your turning chains or a 'fake' double crochet (dc).

These chains count as the first stitch on your new row, so skip the first stitch, bring the yarn over the hook, and insert the hook under both loops of the second stitch from the previous row.

2.
Bring your yarn over your hook again, and pull through the stitch (the first two loops) on your hook.

3.
You now have three loops on your hook. Bring your yarn over your hook again and pull through the first two loops that are on the hook.

4.
Now there are just two loops remaining on your hook. Repeat step 3, bringing your yarn over your hook and pulling through the remaining two loops on the hook.

5.
You now have a single loop remaining on your hook. You have completed a double crochet.

Treble crochet (tr)

As with the other stitches, the method for crocheting the first step of a treble crochet will differ depending on whether it is a first row or a subsequent row. In a first row, you will work into the foundation chain, whereas in a subsequent row, you will work into your previous stitches.

1a.
Work your first row of treble crochet into the foundation chain. Skip the first four stitches, counting from the one nearest the hook. Bring your yarn over your hook and then bring it round a second time so you have two 'yarn overs' on your hook.

Insert your hook into the fifth stitch along as shown. You have to skip more chain stitches than with any of the previous stitches, as the treble crochet is a taller stitch.

1b.
If you are starting a subsequent row, make four chain stitches. These are your turning chains or a 'fake' treble crochet. They count as the first stitch of the new row.

Skip the first stitch of the previous row, bring the yarn over the hook twice, then insert it under both loops of the second stitch.

2.
Bring your yarn over your hook and pull it through the stitch (the first two loops on your hook).

3.
You now have four loops on your hook. Bring the yarn over the hook and pull through the first two loops.

4.
Now there are three loops left on your hook. Bring your yarn over again and pull through the first two loops.

5.
You now have two loops left on your hook. Bring your yarn over your hook for a final time and pull through these loops.

6.
There is now a single loop on your hook and you have completed a treble crochet.

Counting stitches

Having too many or too few stitches in a row can be
a problem for many beginners. A key part of having the
right number of stitches is being able to count them –
if you don't know how many stitches you have crocheted
you won't know whether you have gone wrong.

There are two ways to count how many single crochet,
half-double crochet, double crochet or treble crochet
stitches you have made in a row:

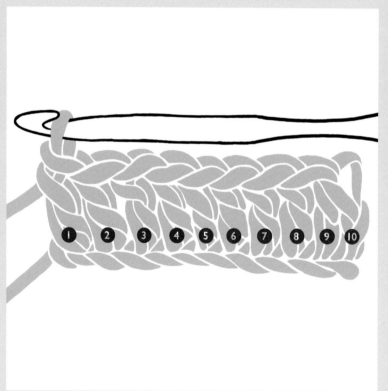

FROM THE SIDE
Count up the long 'posts' of the
stitches. If you are struggling
to do this, try stretching your
crochet piece slightly widthways
so that there are gaps between
your stitches. Don't forget
to count your turning chain
(see page 54, stitch 10 in the
diagram), unless you are doing
single crochet.

FROM THE TOP

Look down onto the 'V' of each stitch. You may find it easier to do this when you are counting single crochet stitches as they are fairly short.

Both methods work equally well, but you may find one easier to see and count than the other. To make sure you are counting correctly, work a row of 20 double crochet stitches and count them from the side, then from the top. Did you count 20 stitches both times? If not go back, count again and work out where you are miscounting.

Turning chains and 'fake' stitches

'Turning chain' is the name given to the chain stitches that you might need to work at the beginning of each new row, or round – these turning chains will always be indicated by a pattern. Their purpose is to create the correct height for the next proper stitch. Making a turning chain at the start of the row ensures your first proper stitches are as tall as they should be, and avoids your crochet looking wonky.

A turning chain counts as your first stitch of the row. This means that once you have crocheted the turning chain, you skip the first stitch of the previous row and crochet into the second stitch. The turning chain will be made up of a certain number of chain stitches, as indicated by the pattern. Sometimes you will see the turning chain referred to as a 'fake' stitch. This is because it looks like a real stitch, and it is going to stand in for one, but it's actually just chain stitches.

To illustrate this with an example, imagine you have a row of 20 double crochet stitches and you're ready for the second row – the pattern should ask you to crochet three chain stitches for your turning chain (these will count as the first double crochet stitch of the new row). You've now got one double crochet 'fake' stitch, and you only need to make 19 more real double crochet stitches to complete the row.

If you are working in single crochet, you won't need to skip a stitch.

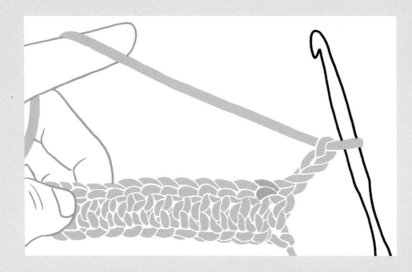

The number of chain stitches you will need depends on which stitch you are crocheting in. Each of the basic crochet stitches is a different height: single crochet being the smallest and double treble the tallest, as shown in the diagram and the list below. For example, if you are crocheting treble crochet stitches, your turning chain will consist of four chain stitches.

Single crochet = 1ch
Half-double crochet = 2ch
Double crochet = 3ch
Treble crochet = 4ch
Double treble crochet = 5ch

	dtr	tr	dc	hdc	sc	slst
ch	5	4	3	2	1	0

This isn't a hard and fast rule. It depends on your tension when chaining: the idea is that the chains end up the same height as your stitch. So, if you make three chains for a double crochet stitch but they end up being taller than your double crochet, you may just want to do one or two. The actual number of chains doesn't matter, it's the height that is important here.

Joining a new yarn

Whether you want to change colour or have just run out of yarn, at some point you will need to swap to a new ball. There are two main ways to join a new yarn. The one you use will depend on what you are making and where you are in the pattern.

THE SLIPSTITCH METHOD

Use this if you are starting a new colour yarn for a new section of crochet. Also use this method if you are continuing with the same ball but are going to work on a different part of the project, for example you could be adding a handle to a bag.

Simply cut and fasten off your current yarn (see page 66). Join the new yarn to your hook and work a slipstitch (see page 64) into the stitch that is your new starting point.

THE CONTINUOUS CROCHET METHOD

This is shown opposite, and it involves using the new yarn to complete the last stitch you are working, which means you don't have to fasten off and rejoin. It gives a nice smooth transition between the two yarns and can be used at any point during a project.

1.
Work the last stitch with your
current yarn as normal, but stop
before you make your last yarn
over and pull through the final
two loops. Drop the working
yarn and make the yarn over
with the new yarn.

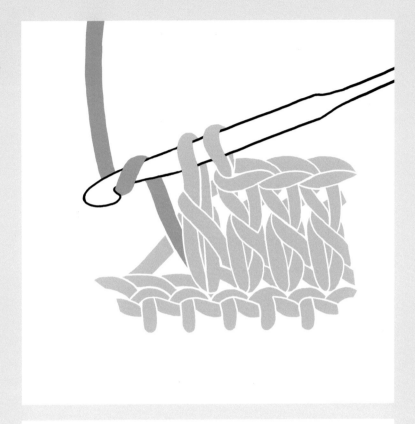

2.
Pull the new yarn through
the two loops on your hook
to complete the stitch. Cut the
old yarn and knot the two tails
together on the wrong side. You
can now continue crocheting as
normal with the new yarn.

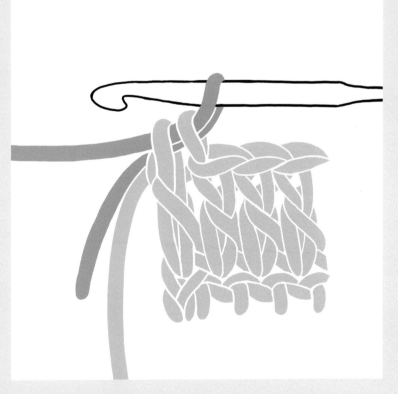

Increase and decrease stitches

Increasing and decreasing the number of stitches in a row or round is how we shape a piece of crochet. By adding more stitches (increasing) you will make your piece larger or wider. Removing stitches (decreasing) makes it smaller or narrower. Once you master this technique, you will be able to tackle items such as amigurumi (those cute little crocheted toys), as well as projects such as clothing that require shaping.

INCREASING

Increasing is very straightforward, as you simply work two stitches into one stitch. The pattern will tell you exactly where to make your increase. For example, the instruction 'Sc in next 2sts, increase', means that you should work one single crochet in each of the next two stitches and two single crochet stitches in the following stitch. This increases the total number of stitches in the row or round. If you started with a row of 12 stitches and worked two increases, you would end up with two extra stitches and have 14 stitches in total.

1a.
For a single crochet increase, work the first stitch as usual.

1b.
Insert your hook through the same stitch in the row below and make a second single crochet, next to the first.

DECREASING

The method for decreasing in crochet involves merging two stitches into one, and it varies depending on which stitch you use. The steps below show you how to decrease in single crochet, because this is most commonly used in work that involves shaping. By working one stitch into two stitches, you will decrease the total number of stitches in the row or round. If you start with 12 stitches in a row and work two decreases, you will have two fewer stitches – a total of 10.

1.
A decrease is worked over two stitches. Insert your hook into the first stitch, bring the yarn over your hook and pull up a loop.

Insert your hook into the second stitch and do the same. You now have three loops on your hook.

2.
Yarn over, and pull through all three loops on your hook.

3.
You have now created a single stitch which goes into the two stitches beneath it.

Working in the round

This section shows you how to work in rounds rather than rows. Instead of turning your work at the end of a row and then working back along the same row, you crochet around a central 'ring' so you always start and end at the same point.

Despite what the name may suggest, working in the round isn't just for making circular items. 'Granny squares' are one of the best examples of this technique. These squares or blocks can be turned into a huge range of projects from blankets to bags and even clothing. The squares for both the block cushion and block blanket (see pages 102 and 104) are worked in the round.

There are two main ways of working in the round.

FOUNDATION RING

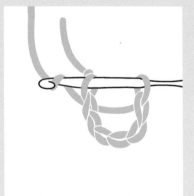 

1.
Crochet a short chain – your pattern will tell you how many stitches to work. Insert your hook through the first stitch you made and pull through both loops on the hook to join into a ring.

2.
Work your first round of stitches into the centre of this ring instead of the top of the chain stitches.

This method is nice and simple, and great for any project as long as you don't mind having a small hole in the centre of your work. For items such as toys (where you don't want any of the stuffing to escape) I use the 'magic ring' method. Once you have done it a few times it will be a piece of cake, but it can take a few attempts to master.

MAGIC RING

 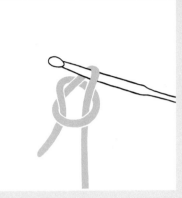

1.
Make a loop with your yarn, with the tail underneath and the working yarn looping over on top. Insert your hook into this loop and hook the working yarn.

2.
Pull the working yarn up through the loop, being careful not to pull too tight and close up the loop.

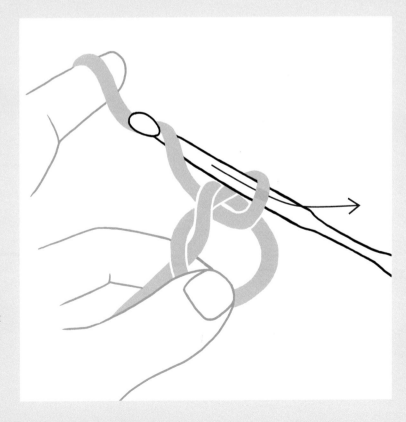

3.
Bring your yarn over your hook and pull it through the loop that is on your hook.

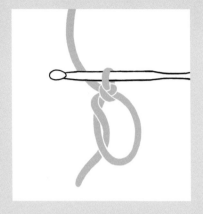

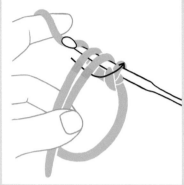

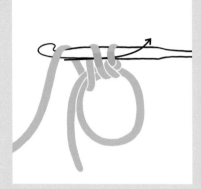

4.
You are now ready to start crocheting into the ring. These diagrams show you how to do this with single crochet stitches.

5.
Hold on to both the yarn tail and the loop as you work, so that the magic ring does not come undone. Insert your hook into the ring, bring your yarn over your hook and pull up a loop.

6.
Yarn over a second time and pull it through both loops on your hook.

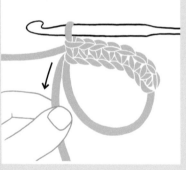

7.
You have crocheted your first single crochet into the magic ring.

8.
Continue working as many stitches as your pattern tells you to. Then pull the yarn tail to close the magic ring. You may need to pull quite firmly to get it to close fully. There should be almost no gap in the centre.

9.
You can now continue crocheting as normal.

Working in a spiral

Almost all amigurumi items are worked in a continuous spiral. This means that there is no visible seam between the rounds on the crochet fabric and the toys have a neat finish from every angle. Instead of working a round and then joining the last stitch to the first one, you complete the last stitch and then go straight on to the first stitch of the new round.

When you are working in a spiral, use a stitch marker (see page 18), or an equivalent tool such as a small safety pin, to mark the start of the row you are working. This will help you keep track of where you are in a pattern if you lose your place or have to undo some of your work. Attach your marker to the first stitch of the round, sliding it under the two loops that make up the top 'V'. Once you have crocheted all the way round and are back to this stitch, take the marker out. Work the first stitch of the new round and then reinsert the marker into the 'V' of the stitch you have just made. This way, you will always know when you are at the beginning of the round, and you can easily keep count of how many rounds you have worked.

Slipstitch (slst)

Slipstitch differs from the other stitches that you have been learning because it is not used to create a crocheted fabric. You would not see a cushion made entirely from slipstitch because it doesn't have any height. Instead, it is a purely functional joining stitch. It is used when you need to add on a new yarn, when working in the round to make a foundation ring, and to join the first and last stitches of each round. Slipstitch is also useful if you need to add a flat edging to a crochet piece and as a quick method to join two pieces.

JOINING A FOUNDATION RING

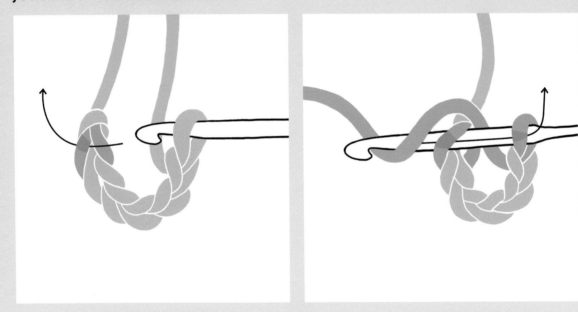

1.
Work the given number of chain stitches, then insert your hook into the first chain you made.

2.
Bring the yarn over your hook, pull the yarn through the chain stitch and then through the loop on your hook.

JOINING TWO CROCHET PIECES

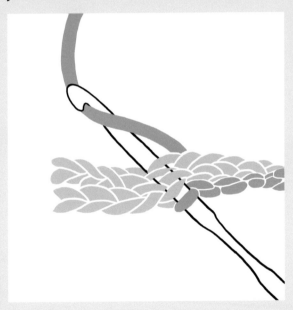
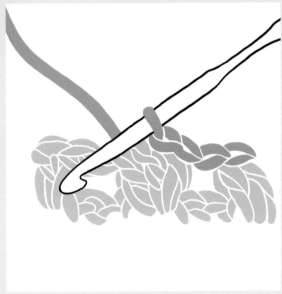

1.
Place the two pieces you are joining together with the corners matching and the right sides facing outwards. Insert your hook through the 'V' at the top of any stitch on the front piece and the 'V' on the corresponding stitch at the back. Bring the yarn over your hook.

2.
Pull the yarn through both stitches and then through the loop on your hook. Repeat this until you reach the end of the seam.

   It's really that simple! Make sure you don't do any extra 'yarn overs' or you may discover you've accidentally worked a single crochet stitch instead of a slipstitch.

Ending your work

Ending a piece you have been crocheting is actually much simpler than you may think. Beginners sometimes feel they need to tie additional knots, but it's really not necessary. Follow these instructions, make sure you weave in your ends securely (see page 78) and your work will be safe from unravelling.

1.
When you have finished your crochet piece, or if you are attaching a new yarn without using the 'continuous crochet' method (see page 56) you will need to fasten off your work.

Start by cutting the yarn, leaving a tail of about 15cm (6in), or more if your pattern asks you to. Sometimes you will need a longer tail so you can use it to stitch parts of your work together.

2.
Bring the yarn tail over your hook and pull it through the loop as if you were making a chain stitch.

3.
Instead of stopping once the yarn is through, keep pulling with your hook until the whole tail has passed through the loop. Give the end a little tug to tighten off the final stitch and you are all done.

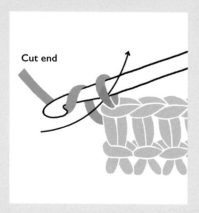

Cut end

STITCH AND TECHNIQUE LIBRARY

Tension and sample swatches

In the section about holding your hook and your yarn (see pages 30–1), I mentioned tension and why it is so important in crochet. Keeping an even tension throughout will give your work a neat and professional finish, but every crocheter has a slightly different tension – just as everyone has different handwriting. There isn't really a right or wrong tension (unless your work is extremely loose or extremely tight), but patterns are often written to measurements based on the designer's own tension. This is especially important for items such as clothing that have to be a specific size. If your tension is very different to the one the pattern intends, then the item may end up too big or too small.

How do you know if your tension is the same as the pattern? Well, any pattern that has to be made to an exact size (such as clothing) will ask you to crochet a sample swatch. It will give you the number of stitches and rows to crochet, followed by the finished shape, for example: '12sc by 10 rows = 10 × 10cm (4 × 4in)'. This means if you make up a swatch that is 12 single crochets across and 10 rows high, using the recommended yarn and hook, it should come out at 10cm (4in) square.

If your piece ends up bigger than the given dimensions, it means your tension is too loose, so you will need to go down a half, or whole, hook size. If your sample ends up smaller, then your tension is too tight and you should use a larger hook. Make another sample swatch with your new hook and keep changing as necessary, until you have the correct measurements.

Keeping your work straight

There are several things I hear over and over again from students who have been having difficulties with their crochet. The two most common are: 'my edges are wonky', and 'my piece gets wide and then narrow – and then wide again!' Both of these problems are caused by not having enough stitches in a row, meaning you have skipped stitches somewhere, or from having too many stitches, meaning you have worked a few extras along the way.

One reason that beginners end up with the wrong number of stitches is that it can sometimes be hard to see exactly where you should make your next stitch. It can also be tricky to tell whether you have already worked a stitch in a particular loop. There is no magic answer or secret crochet trick to this – it just comes from practice and from looking closely at your crochet.

<u>To prevent skipping stitches</u>
Take your time and try to avoid distractions. If you are having a conversation while crocheting, or you are rushing to finish a row, you are much more likely to skip over a stitch.

<u>To prevent adding extra stitches</u>
Try to resist the temptation of going for the nice big easy-to-see stitch. Any stitch you have just worked into will have been stretched a bit by your hook, so you may have already crocheted into it.

It is also a good idea to stop after each row or round and count how many stitches you have made. Compare that figure to the number of stitches you are supposed to have. It takes a bit of time but makes such a difference, as you will be able to identify a problem as soon as it occurs instead of realizing five rows later.

You can also get an incorrect number of stitches if you don't skip a stitch at the start of the row or do not work into the final stitch. For example, say you are working rows of double crochet and you should have 20 double crochet stitches but you end up with 21. The pattern said 'Ch3 (counts as first dc). Skip first st, dc in each st.'

This means that you should start with three chain stitches which become a 'fake' double crochet and count as your first double crochet stitch (see page 48). So you already have one double crochet stitch, but there are still 20 stitches to go. If you worked into each of them you would have 21 double crochets, including the 'fake' stitch from the beginning. To avoid gaining an extra stitch, work into the second stitch instead of the first. You will end up with 19 double crochet stitches, plus the 'fake' double crochet. That adds up to 20, so now you would have the correct number of stitches.

In this same example, if you only have 19 stitches, the most common reason is that you haven't worked into the last stitch of the row. It may look as if you have, but the final stitch is actually your 'fake' double crochet (the three chain stitches) from the row below. This often sits slightly lower down and to the side, so it doesn't always look like you should be crocheting into it. Work your final double crochet of the row into the third chain stitch (the one nearest the top) of this 'fake' double crochet.

Decorative stitches

Using decorative stitches in your crochet work helps add interest and texture to a piece, and it is a great way of building up your skills. There are hundreds of stitches out there, and some are more complicated than others. Here are a few of my favourites, which are relatively easy to pick up once you have mastered the crochet basics.

WAFFLE

Foundation chain: Start with an even number of ch.

Row 1: Hdc in second ch from the hook, hdc in each ch to end.

R2: Ch1, hdc in first stitch. *Hdc into BLO of next st, hdc into FLO of next stitch. Repeat from * to end, finishing with a normal hdc in the last st. (See page 39 for BLO and FLO.)

Repeat Row 2 as many times as required.

LINEN

Foundation chain: Start with an even number of ch.

Row 1: Sc in second ch from hook. *Ch1, skip next ch, sc in next ch. Repeat from * to end.

R2: Ch1, skip first st. *Sc into ch1 space from the previous row, ch1, skip next sc. Repeat from * to end, finishing with 1sc in the last ch.

Repeat Row 2 as many times as required, always ending with 1sc in the first ch from the previous row. This may be tricky to find at first, but is essential to keeping your edges straight.

STAR

Foundation chain: Start with an even number of ch.

Row 1: Insert hook in second ch from hook. Yarn over (yo), pull up a loop and keep it on hook. Repeat this process in the next 4ch, so that you have 6 loops on your hook. Yo and pull through all 6 loops, slst to close star. This is your first star stitch.

The next star stitch is worked along the edge of your first star and into the next 2ch. To make the 5 loops you will need to insert your hook through the previous stitches where shown, pulling up the yarn at each point and keeping it on your hook.

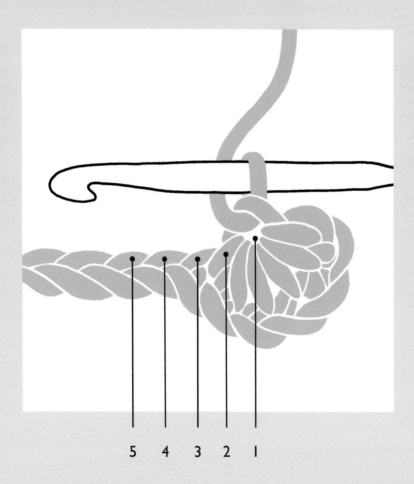

5   4   3   2   1

*Insert hook
(1) through the centre of the previous star stitch, yo and pull up
(2) between the last 2 loops of the previous star stitch, yo and pull up
(3) in the same ch as loop 5 of your previous star stitch
(4) in the next ch, yo and pull up
(5) in the next ch, yo and pull up.
This may sound complicated, but just focus on one loop at a time and use the diagram for reference. Once you've done it a few times you'll get into a rhythm.

When you have finished, you will have 6 loops on your hook. Yo and pull through all 6 loops, slst to close star. You've now completed your second star stitch. Repeat from * to the end. Hdc in the last ch (the same st as loop 5 of the star).

R2: Ch2 (counts as 1hdc). 2hdc into the centre of each star stitch from the previous row. Hdc in the last st.

R3: Ch3. Insert hook in second ch from hook, yo and pull up a loop. Repeat in next ch along the next 3hdc, each time pulling up a loop. You will have 6 loops on your hook. Yo and pull through all 6 loops, slst to close star. This is your first star stitch of the row.

To complete the row, repeat from * on Row 1 to the end. Hdc in last stitch of the row (the same hdc as loop 5 of the star).

Repeat Rows 2–3 as many times as required.

LEMON PEEL

Foundation chain: Start with an odd number of ch.

Row 1: Sc in second ch from hook. *Dc in next chain, sc in next ch. Repeat from * to the end, dc in the last ch.

R2: Ch1. Sc in first dc. *Dc in next sc, sc in next dc. Repeat from * to the end, dc in last sc.

Repeat Row 2 as many times as required.

CRUNCH

Foundation chain: Start with an odd number of stitches.

Row 1: Slst in second ch from hook. *Hdc in next ch, slst in next ch. Repeat from * to the end, hdc in last ch.

R2: Ch1, slst in first hdc. *Hdc in next slst, slst in next hdc. Repeat from * to the end, hdc in last slst.

Repeat Row 2 as many times as required.

STITCH AND TECHNIQUE LIBRARY

Finishing your work

WEAVING IN ENDS

Let's be honest, when you have spent hours (and hours) crocheting a beautiful item, sewn the pieces together and added those finishing touches, it's very tempting to reach for the scissors and snip off the yarn ends rather than weaving them in. But please don't – given all the time you have put into your crochet project, you don't want it to unravel. Weaving in your ends prevents this from happening.

1. Thread the yarn end through a darning or yarn needle and run it through the back of a few stitches on the wrong side of your work.

2. Sew the thread in one direction, back the opposite way and then go in the original direction again. You don't have to weave in the whole tail, but it is important to change direction. Don't pull on the yarn end too much as this will distort your work. Make sure you only go through the stitches that are the same colour as your yarn tail, as it's much easier to hide yarn in matching crochet fabric.

3. Use scissors to snip the remaining yarn close to the stitches.

STITCH AND TECHNIQUE LIBRARY

BLOCKING WORK

Blocking is the process of pinning your finished crochet work, then applying moisture or steam to shape it and give it a neat finish.

I don't block many of my projects, particularly if they will be stretched and pulled about anyway, or if they don't really benefit from being blocked. Amigurumi toys, for example, don't need blocking as their stuffing gives them shape and structure. Granny squares hold their shape well, and when they are joined together they keep their neat square shape. Acrylic yarns should not be blocked, as heat and steam can damage the fibres.

But if you are crocheting clothing, particularly more fitted garments, I recommend blocking your pieces before joining them together to ensure a good fit. Also, if you finish a crochet piece and it does not sit flat, or looks a bit wonky in places, it could benefit from being blocked.

There are several methods of blocking, but I've found this process works best and doesn't require lots of extra materials.

1. Cover an area of an ironing board (or you could do this on a carpet or rug) with a plastic sheet, making sure the part covered is slightly larger than the item you are blocking.

2. Pin your piece down using large rust-proof dressmaking pins. Place the pins at regular intervals around the edges. Be careful not to overstretch the crochet or pull it out of shape.

3. Use a spray bottle to spray the whole piece with water. Ensure your crochet is wet through but not too soaked.

4. Leave until fully dry. This may mean overnight, depending on the yarn type and the temperature in the room. Remove the pins, and you are all done.

JOINING PIECES TOGETHER

There are many ways to join your finished pieces together, depending on the result you are after. You can use the method below for any project. Once you've mastered this and are feeling more confident, you can find other methods in books or online to add to your repertoire. You can try the slipstitch method on page 65 too.

1. Begin by threading a yarn needle with a length of yarn. Your stitches will be mostly hidden, but it's still a good idea to choose a colour that matches the pieces you are joining. Tie the yarn to the first stitch on one edge.

2. Line up the two pieces with their right sides facing, so the stitches along both edges match up.

3. Sew through the first stitch on one edge and then the first stitch on the other, then through the second stitch on each piece. Pull the yarn gently until the edges sit close together and there's no gap between them. Continue until you reach the end of the seam.

4. Sew twice through the final stitch, then tie the working yarn to the loop you have just sewn. Finish off by weaving in the ends (see page 78).

ADDING BORDERS

Borders are a great way of adding a neat and regular finish to your work, as well as giving it an extra decorative trim. They can also help even out the shape of a piece, as well as hiding a number of mistakes such as irregular sides. Although it can be tempting to skip the step of adding a border, particularly on a large project such as a blanket, it really does make a huge difference.

In the same way that there are hundreds of crochet stitches, there are also hundreds of different borders. Here are a few of my favourite borders.

Simple border
The most basic border (shown opposite) is made by crocheting around the edges of your work with a single crochet stitch. You can do as many rounds as you like to make the border narrow or wide, depending on the look you are going for. Decorative borders often start with a round of single crochet to give an even base, before other stitches are added.

1. Start by joining on the yarn with a slipstitch. You can do this anywhere on the edge of your piece, but I usually start in a corner. When crocheting along the top and bottom edges, work one single crochet into each stitch.

2. Take care when you come to the side edges. Here you will be working into the ends of your rows, and there will be lots of random spaces you could crochet into. Working out how many stitches you will need involves a bit of trial and error. Try to keep them evenly spaced – if you make too many, too close together, you will notice the border starting to bunch up and ripple. This means you need to space your stitches out a bit more. If you don't make enough stitches, your crochet piece will bunch up as the tight border pulls it out of shape. This means you need to make your stitches more closely together.

3. When you reach a corner, you will need to crochet extra stitches to go round it. I usually do two or three stitches in the last stitch of one side, and the first stitch of the next side. Again, this takes practice. Keep checking to ensure your work is lying flat.

Picot border
If you are after something a bit fancier, the picot edging looks much more complicated than it is, plus it is great for adding extra interest and texture. The little bobbly points are made by doubling over a short row of chain stitches. Experiment with different numbers of chains to give different size picots.

Row 1: Sc all around.

Row 2: *Ch3, sc in second ch from hook, skip 1sc, 1sc in next st. Repeat from * all round.

Scalloped border

This cute and dainty border is probably one of my favourites. It is perfect for kids' items or for turning a plain blanket or cushion into something special. The rounded scallops are created by making five double crochets in the same space, so although they look advanced they're actually pretty straightforward.

Row 1: Sc all around.

Round 2: Sc in first st, *skip next st, 5dc in next st, skip next st, sc in next st. Repeat from * all around.

MAKING POMPOMS AND TASSELS

One of the simplest ways of adding a finishing flourish to your crochet is with pompoms or tassels. They're both really fun to make and a great way to use up any leftover yarn. Once you have learned how to make a basic pompom and tassel, you can experiment with making multicoloured versions or using different types or weight of yarn.

<u>Making a pompom</u>

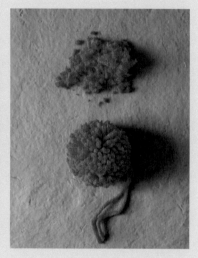

1.
Open up the pompom maker. Wrap your yarn round one half until it's completely full. Close that half and open up the other side. Cover this side with yarn until it's full and then close it into the middle again.

2.
Cut through all the layers of yarn on both sides, following the groove on the maker with a pair of scissors.

3.
Take a length of yarn and tie it securely around the centre of the pompom maker, making sure it goes between the two halves. Pull the ends as tightly as you can and tie them in a secure knot. Open the pompom maker and pull the two halves apart. Trim the pompom to neaten it up, but leave the long yarn tails. You will use these to sew the pompom to your project.

Making a tassel

1. Take a piece of thick card that is a bit longer than you want your finished tassel to be or cut a piece to size. Wrap your yarn around the length of the card as many times as you like. The more times you wrap, the thicker your tassel will be.

2. Once you are happy with the thickness, cut a length of yarn and use your hand to slide it under the loops at one end. Tie it in a secure knot to hold the strands together, then cut through the loops at the other end.

3. Remove the card. Approximately one inch from the top of the tassel (where you secured the strands with a knot), wrap another piece of yarn around the strands. Tie this piece of yarn tightly.

4. Give the ends of your tassel a trim or leave them as they are if you prefer. Stitch your finished tassel on to your project.

Projects

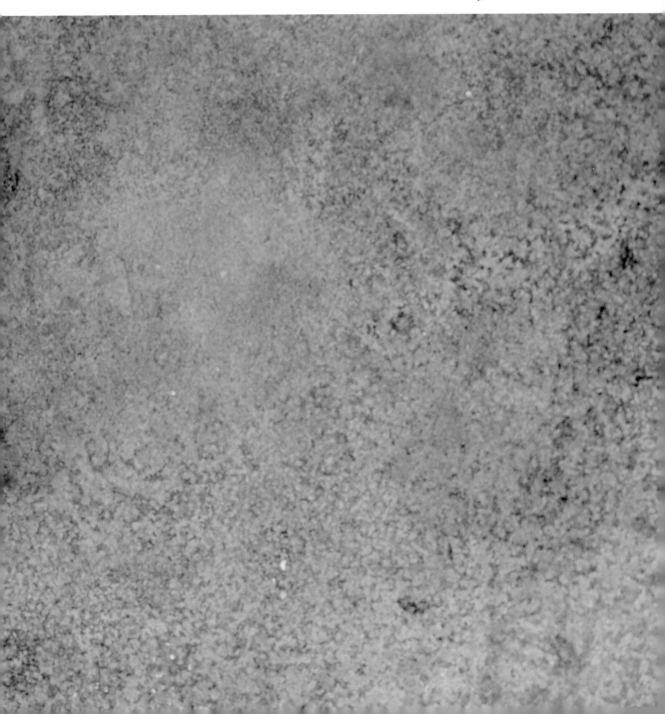

Ear warmer

Looking at these snuggly ear warmers, no one would guess this is the simplest project in the book. Constructed from two rectangles of single crochet, they are not only a really easy make, they are also very quick to whip up. This is great because once you start wearing yours, it won't be long before family and friends ask you to make ear warmers for them too! These examples have been worked in single crochet, but you could also try making them from decorative stitches. The stitch I used for the bobble cushion (see page 112) would make a lovely textured ear warmer.

YOU WILL NEED
Paintbox Simply Chunky yarn:
   1 × 100g (3½-oz.) ball in Mustard
   Yellow or Vanilla Cream
6mm hook
Scissors
Yarn needle

SIZE
53cm circumference × 7.5cm wide
   (21in circumference × 3in wide)

Main section

Start by making the main part of the ear warmer. This is the band that will go around your head.

Foundation chain: Ch65.
After you have worked 65 chain stitches check that the length is correct for your head (or the head of whomever the ear warmer is for). Remember the final piece will have a bit of stretch to it, so your foundation chain should fit snugly around the head. If necessary, add or remove a few stitches until it's the correct size before you begin Row 1.

Row 1: Sc in second ch from hook, sc in each ch to end. (64sts)

R2: Ch1. Sc in first st and each st to end.
The first ch1 doesn't count as a stitch when you are working in single crochet, so you will need to work into every stitch along the row. Count your stitches every few rows to make sure you still have the same number that you started with – this will always be one stitch fewer than you chained at the start.

R3–13: Repeat Row 2. Fasten off leaving a 30cm (12in) tail.
You can make your ear warmer wider by continuing to work more rows in the same way, instead of stopping at Row 13. If you add a lot more rows you may need to make your centre section (see next page) a tiny bit longer so it will fit around the band.

Project continues overleaf

PROJECTS

Centre section

Now make the band that will gather your ear warmer at the front. It's just a small rectangle, worked in the same way as the main section.

Foundation Chain: Ch12.

Row 1: Sc in second ch from hook, sc in each ch to end. (11sts)

R2: Ch1. Sc into each st to end.

R3: Repeat Row 2. Fasten off leaving a 20cm (8in) tail.

Finishing your ear warmer

Start by weaving in the short yarn ends on both sections (see page 78). Thread the remaining long tail on the main section through a yarn needle. Use this to sew the two short edges together (see page 81), making sure to match them up so they sit neatly. Weave in the remaining yarn. You now have a band of crochet. Wrap the centre section over the join you have just created so that it covers the stitches. Use the tail to sew the short edges together, on the wrong side, then weave in the end.

Cup cozy

One of the very first things I crocheted was a cup cozy. It's such a simple project, but can easily be adapted and resized. And, perhaps most importantly, it is a useful item. Over the years I've amassed quite a collection of cup cozies and always have at least one in my bag. They also make a great gift when paired with a ceramic cup and a box of fancy herbal tea.

YOU WILL NEED
Rico Baby Classic DK yarn:
  1 × 50g (1¾-oz.) ball in Melon
  1 × 50g (1¾-oz.) ball in Steel Grey
  (One ball makes 3–4 cozies)
4mm hook
Scissors
Yarn needle
Cup (check the measurements
  before you begin)

SIZE
21.5cm circumference × 6cm tall
  (8½in circumference × 2½in tall)

The cozy will fit a standard
  takeaway coffee cup, but you
  can alter the foundation ring
  to fit a different sized cup.

Foundation ring: Ch41. Join with slst in first ch.
Slip the ring onto your cup, making sure you have a snug fit as the chain stitches will stretch slightly. You may need to undo the slst and add or remove a few stitches before you move on to Round 1.

Round 1: Ch1. Sc in each ch around. Join with slst in first sc. (40sts)

R2: Ch1. Sc in each sc around. Join with slst in first sc.
Technically you are crocheting in rounds. Work in the same way as you would if you were crocheting in rows, but without turning. When you get back to the beginning, make a slipstitch into the first single crochet stitch to join the round.

R3–14: Repeat Round 2. Fasten off.
You are essentially just repeating Round 2 another 12 times – remember to join the ends of each round. You can make your cup cozy taller or shorter by working more or fewer rounds.

Finishing your cup cozy

Simply weave in the two ends (see page 78). You could then embellish the cozy with appliqué – I love cutting motifs from felt and stitching them on. Alternatively, you could sew on some carefully selected buttons or trims. Of course, they are also beautiful just left as they are.

Ribbed pompom hat

Although the ribbed texture of this hat makes it look as if it's been knitted, it is in fact crocheted using a very simple trick. Once you've mastered working in the back loop only (known as BLO – see page 39) this pattern works up quickly, especially when using Super Chunky yarn and a large hook, as I have done. Hats may seem intimidating, but this one starts off as a simple rectangle made up of rows of half-double crochet – definitely nothing to be afraid of!

YOU WILL NEED
Paintbox Wool Mix Super
    Chunky yarn:
    2 × 100g (3½-oz.) balls in
    Vanilla Cream
10mm hook
Extra yarn for a pompom (if you'd
    like to make it in a different colour)
Pompom maker
Scissors
Yarn needle

SIZE
The pattern shows you how
    to adjust the size to achieve
    the right fit.

Foundation chain: Ch21 + 2.
You can chain any number you like – the length of the foundation chain will be the height of your hat so the more stitches, the taller your hat. The 'plus two' chain stitches are the turning chain or 'fake' hdc (see page 54).

Row 1: Hdc in fourth ch from hook. Hdc in each ch to end. (21sts)
You start in the fourth chain from your hook because the first two chains are your 'fake' hdc. The third chain acts as the foundation chain stitch for the fake hdc, so you skip the first three chains.

R2: Ch2 (counts as first hdc). Skip first st, hdc into BLO of each st to end.
You skip the first stitch here because it is the one that the 'fake' hdc or turning chain comes out of. If you crocheted into every stitch of the previous row you'd end up with 21 hdc plus your 'fake' hdc. And if you did this on every row you'd gain one stitch each time, and your work would gradually get wider and wider.

R3–26: Repeat Row 2. Fasten off leaving a 90cm (1 yard) tail.
My hat has 26 rows, but you can easily adjust this. Hold your work up to your head regularly to check the size – you can crochet more or fewer rows so it fits you snugly. Remember your hat will stretch as you wear it so don't make it loose to start off with.

Project continues overleaf

RIBBED POMPOM HAT

Finishing your hat

Weave in the short tail, then thread the long tail through your yarn needle. Bring together the two short edges of your work, with the right sides facing, to form a tube. Match up the stitches along each edge and sew them together (see page 81).

Fasten off the yarn at the end of the seam, but don't cut it yet – you are now going to gather the top edge to make the tube into a hat. Pass the needle through the raised ridge of each ribbed section all the way round, then pull the yarn up like a drawstring. Sew a few large stitches across the top of the gathered section to secure the gathers.

Make a pompom with the remaining, or contrast, yarn (see page 84). Use the two long tails that you tied it up with to sew it onto your hat.

Ribbed pompom scarf

By using the same technique as in the ribbed pompom hat (see page 94), but changing the number of stitches and rows, you can create many other crocheted items including this matching scarf. I love long scarves that I can wrap round a few times, so I've crocheted lots of rows, but you can easily adjust the length to suit you. Remember that the number of chain stitches you start with will determine the width of your scarf and the number of rows will determine the length.

Foundation chain: Ch150 + 2.

Row 1: Hdc into fourth ch from hook. Hdc into each ch to end. (150sts)

R2: Ch2 (counts as first hdc). Skip first st, hdc into BLO of each st to end.

R3–10: Repeat Row 2. Fasten off.

YOU WILL NEED
Paintbox Wool Mix Super
    Chunky yarn:
    6 × 100g (3½-oz.) balls in
    Slate Grey
10mm hook
Extra yarn for pompoms (if you'd
    like to make them in a
    different colour)
Pompom maker
Scissors
Yarn needle

SIZE
15cm × 260cm (6in × 102in)

Finishing your scarf

Weave in the two yarn tails (see page 78). Your scarf is now ready to use as it is, but there are a few options for finishing it if you'd like to. Sew the two short edges together in the same way as for the ribbed pompom hat (see page 96) to create an infinity scarf. Alternatively, you can sew a matching pompom to each corner (as I have done). Finally, you can fold in the two corners of one end to create a point and stitch them together. Finish by sewing a pompom to the point and repeat on the other end.

RIBBED POMPOM SCARF

Colour block squares

Although I've been crocheting for nearly fifteen years, I still love crocheting blocks (independently crocheted squares). It's the perfect on-the-go project, as you can make items such as throws without having to carry the whole thing around with you. Simply crochet a few blocks on your morning commute, or while waiting for an appointment, then leave them at home once they are done. Make some each day and soon you'll have enough for a cushion, a blanket or much more.

The pattern below is for a solid crochet square. On the following pages you'll find instructions for turning a stack of them into either a floor cushion or a blanket. You can create so many different results by playing with the yarn type, colours, hook size and the number of squares you use, not to mention joining them in different ways, adding borders and even embellishing with tassels and pompoms.

BASIC COLOUR BLOCK

Foundation ring: Ch4. Join with slst in first ch.
This makes a little circle of stitches, which you will work into on Round 1.

Round 1: Ch3. 2dc into ring. *Ch2, 3dc into ring. Repeat from * twice more. Ch2, join with slst in top of ch3.
You will now have four clusters of three double crochet stitches, with two chain stitches in between each cluster.

R2: Slst in next 3 sts. Ch3, 1dc into space. Ch2, 2dc into same space. *1dc in each of next 3sts, 2dc into next space, ch2, 2dc into same space. Repeat from * twice more, 1dc in each of next 3sts. Join with slst in top of ch3.
You start the round with slipstitches in the first three stitches so that you can begin your 'proper' crochet stitches in the corner space. These slipstitches allow you to move across the block, but be careful not to work them too tightly or you'll struggle to get your hook into them.

R3: Slst in next 2sts. Ch3, 1dc into space. Ch2, 2dc into same space. *1dc in each of next 7sts. 2dc into next space, ch2, 2dc into same space. Repeat from * twice more, 1dc in each of next 7sts. Join with slst in top of ch3. Fasten off and weave in ends.
Once you've got the hang of how these blocks work up, it's easy to see how to add additional rounds. The pattern will be the same but you will have to work more double crochet stitches along each side, between the corner chain spaces.

Colour block floor cushion

Oversized cushions are perfect for getting cozy with, and for this one I have gone bold with a splash of bright yellow and large areas of solid colour. You can make any size or shape of cushion by purchasing a square or rectangular pad, then crocheting enough squares to cover each side with a snug fit.

YOU WILL NEED
Paintbox Wool Mix Chunky yarn:
  3 × 100g (3½-oz.) balls in
  Blush Pink
  3 × 100g (3½-oz.) balls in
  Champagne White
  2 × 100g (3½-oz.) balls in
  Buttercup Yellow
8mm hook
Scissors
Yarn needle
62cm × 62cm (24in × 24in)
  square cushion pad

SIZE
62cm × 62cm (24in × 24in)

Make 50 basic colour block squares (see page 100):
20 in Blush Pink
18 in Champagne White
12 in Buttercup Yellow

Assembling your cushion

For the front panel, lay out half the squares in five rows of five. Start at the top with two rows of Blush Pink, then add three more rows, each of three Champagne White squares followed by two in Buttercup Yellow. Stitch the squares together (see page 81) using a length of Champagne White and a yarn needle. Join them in rows across, then join the long edges of the rows. Make the back panel in exactly the same way.

Place the front and back panels together with the wrong sides facing and the Buttercup Yellow and Blush Pink squares lined up at one edge. Fasten the Champagne White yarn to one corner with a slipstitch and join three sides of the cover with single crochet (see page 82). Insert your hook under the top of the stitch on one panel, and under the corresponding stitch on the other panel, before working each stitch as normal. Slip your cushion pad inside the cover and crochet along the fourth and final side. Join with a slst in the first stitch and weave in any loose ends.

Colour block blanket

One of my favourite things to crochet is a blanket made up of square blocks. There are so many possible colour and pattern combinations to experiment with. For this blanket I've used cream with pops of colour scattered throughout, but you can crochet your blocks in any colours and arrange them however you like. You could try stripes, or group your blocks to create 2 × 2 squares. Alternatively, you could also arrange them in concentric rectangles. The possibilities are endless, so don't be afraid to experiment.

YOU WILL NEED
Paintbox Simply Chunky yarn:
   4 × 100g (3½-oz.) balls in
   Champagne White
   1 × 100g (3½-oz.) ball in
   Mustard Yellow
   1 × 100g (3½-oz.) ball in
   Peach Orange
   1 × 100g (3½-oz.) ball in
   Stormy Grey
   1 × 100g (3½-oz.) ball in
   Duck Egg Blue
   1 × 100g (3½-oz.) ball in
   Lipstick Pink
6mm hook
Scissors
Yarn needle

SIZE
75cm × 97cm (29in × 38in)

Crochet 63 basic colour block squares (see page 100):
29 in Champagne White
8 in Mustard Yellow, Peach Orange and Stormy Grey
6 in Duck Egg Blue
4 in Lipstick Pink

Assembling your blanket

Lay out the squares in nine rows of seven, based on the arrangement in the photo or in your own design. Use Champagne White yarn and a yarn needle to stitch them together (see page 81). Once joined, slipstitch the Champagne White yarn to any edge stitch, with the right side of the blanket facing you. Work two rounds of single crochet all round the blanket to give it a nice neat border (see page 82). Weave in any loose ends.

Gadget and glasses cases

You may not be able to tell by looking at them, but these cases are worked in the round. You can easily adapt the size to fit any item you like. Why not make a larger version for a tablet or even a laptop? Simply start with a foundation chain that is slightly shorter than the width of your item, to ensure a snug fit, and keep working rounds of single crochet until the case is tall enough.

YOU WILL NEED

Stylecraft Special DK yarn:
  1 × 100g (3½-oz.) ball in Grey
  1 × 100g (3½-oz.) ball in Shrimp
  1 × 100g (3½-oz.) ball in Teal
4mm hook
Stitch marker
Scissors
Yarn needle
Strip of hook-and-loop tape
Sewing needle and matching thread

SIZES

Phone/glasses case
7cm × 16.5cm (2¾in × 6½in)
Gadget case
11.5cm × 16.5cm (4½in × 6½in)

GLASSES CASE

Foundation chain: Ch15 using Grey.

Round 1: Skip first ch. Sc in each of next 13ch, 3sc in last ch. Working into the other side of the chain, sc in each of next 13ch, sc2 in last st. (31sts)
Start by working along the top of the foundation chain as normal and make three single crochet in the final chain stitch. Instead of crocheting back into the stitches you have just made, go around the end and work into the loops at the bottom edge of your foundation chain without turning it over. This produces an oval shape.

R2–27: Sc in each st around.
Now that you are working 'in the round' as normal, use a stitch marker so you know when you have completed each round. There will be no more increases so the piece will stay the same width, but it will get taller as you add more rows.

Change to Teal (see page 56).

R28–37: Sc in each st around. Fasten off.

Flap fastening

Row 1: Rejoin yarn (see page 56) with a slst to the third st from the edge. 1ch, sc in each of next 7sts.

R2–6: Sc in each st. (7sts)

Project continues overleaf

PROJECTS

R7: Decrease, sc in each of next 3sts, decrease. (5sts)

R8: Sc in each st.

R9: Decrease, sc in next st, decrease. Fasten off.

R10: Rejoin the yarn to bottom corner of flap and slst all the way around the flap. Fasten off.

GADGET CASE

Foundation chain: Ch20 using Shrimp.

Round 1: Skip first ch, sc in each of next 18ch, 3sc in last ch. Working into the other side of the chain, sc in each of next 18ch, sc2 in last st. (41sts)

R3–17: Sc in each st around.

Change to Grey (see page 56).

R18–38: Sc in each st around. Fasten off.

Flap fastening

Row 1: Rejoin your yarn with a slst to the 7th st from the edge. 1ch, sc in each of next 9sts.

R2–6: Sc in each st. (9sts)

R7: Decrease, sc in each of next 5sts, decrease. (7sts)

R8: Sc in each st.

R9: Decrease, sc in each of next 3sts, decrease. (5sts)

R10: Decrease, sc in next st, decrease. Fasten off.

R11: Rejoin the yarn to bottom corner of flap and slst all the way around the flap. Fasten off.

Finishing your cases

Weave in all the ends neatly (see page 78). Cut a piece of hook-and-loop tape to size so that it fits on the flap fastening and separate the two parts. Using matching sewing thread and a needle, stitch the soft side of the hook-and-loop tape to the flap fastening and the rough, hooked side to your case in the corresponding spot.

Washcloths

Once you've mastered the basic crochet stitches, the next step is to try out some of the more decorative versions. Making these cloths is a great way to get the hang of them. Working in straight rows means you can focus on learning the stitch itself, rather than simultaneously trying to follow the shaping of a complicated pattern such as a jumper.

The cloths can be used as dishcloths or washcloths, are quick to work up and only require a small amount of yarn. They make a great eco-friendly alternative to mass-produced cloths because they can be washed and reused over and over again.

Instructions for how to crochet all five stitches can be found on pages 72–6. Each stitch has a different appearance and texture, and in addition to working well for cloths, they could easily be used for other projects in the book, such as the ear warmer on page 88.

YOU WILL NEED
Paintbox Cotton Aran yarn:
  1 × 50g (1¾-oz.) ball in Light Caramel
  1 × 50g (1¾-oz.) ball in Mustard Yellow
  1 × 50g (1¾-oz.) ball in Blush Pink
  1 × 50g (1¾-oz.) ball in Peach Orange
  1 × 50g (1¾-oz.) ball in Misty Grey
4.5mm hook
Scissors
Yarn needle

SIZE
15cm × 18cm (6in × 7in) approx.

CRUNCH STITCH CLOTH
Using Light Caramel, ch23 for a foundation chain and work 29 rows in total.

LINEN STITCH CLOTH
Using Mustard Yellow, ch22 for a foundation chain and work 29 rows in total.

WAFFLE STITCH CLOTH
Using Blush Pink, ch24 for a foundation chain and work 16 rows in total.

STAR STITCH CLOTH
Using Peach Orange, ch28 for a foundation chain and work 26 rows in total.

LEMON PEEL STITCH CLOTH
Using Misty Grey, ch23 for a foundation chain and work 27 rows in total.

Finishing your cloths

Work a border around the edge of each cloth in single crochet (see page 82). I used the same yarn as used for the cloth itself, but you could change colour to have a contrasting edge. Fasten off and weave in the ends (see page 78).

Bobble cushions

The bobble effect on these cushions is a simple way of adding texture to your crochet and, when worked in this super chunky yarn, it gives a modern feel to any item. Although it looks complicated, it's actually quite straightforward and the instructions below show you how it works.

YOU WILL NEED

Yarn and Colors Urban yarn:
  3 × 200g (7-oz.) balls in Peach
  4 × 200g (7-oz.) balls in Soft Grey
10mm hook
Scissors
Yarn needle
50cm × 30cm (20in × 12in) pad
  for peach cushion
40cm × 40cm (16in × 16in) pad
  for grey cushion

SIZES

Peach cushion
50cm × 28cm (20in × 11in)
Grey cushion
38cm × 38cm (15in × 15in)

BOBBLE STITCH (BBS)

1. Yarn over and insert hook into the stitch. Yarn over and pull up a loop.

2. Yarn over and pull through the first two loops on your hook.

3. Repeat steps 1–2 three more times. You will end up with five loops on your hook.

4. Yarn over and pull through all five loops. You have now completed a bobble stitch! The bobbles will form on the opposite side, so flip your work over once you've finished so that you can admire them.

PEACH CUSHION

Front panel

Foundation chain: Ch16.

Row 1: Sc in second ch from hook, sc in each ch to end. (15sts)

R2: Ch1. BBS into first st. *Sc in next st, BBS into next st. Repeat from * to end, finishing with a BBS in the last st.

R3: Ch1. Sc in first st and each st to end.

R4: Ch1. Sc in first st. *BBS into next st, sc into next st. Repeat from * to end, finishing with a sc in the final st.
In this row the bobbles are offset from the previous row, so they will sit in between the bobbles from row 2.

Project continues overleaf

R5: Ch1. Sc in first st and each st to end.

R6: Ch1. BBS into first st, *Sc in next st, BBS into next st. Repeat from * to end, finishing with a BBS in the last st.

R7–24: Ch1. Sc in first st and each st to end.

R25: Ch1. BBS into first st. *Sc in next st, BBS into next st. Repeat from * to end, finishing with a BBS in the last st.

R26: Ch1. Sc in first st and each st to end.

R27: Ch1. Sc in first st. *BBS into next st, sc in next st. Repeat from * to end, finishing with a sc in the last st.

R28: Ch1. Sc in first st and each st to end.

R29: Ch1. BBS into first st. *Sc in next st, BBS into next st. Repeat from * to end, finishing with a BBS in the last st.

R30: Ch1. Sc in first st and each st to end. Fasten off and weave in ends.

Back panel

Foundation chain: Ch16.

Row 1: Sc in second ch from hook, sc in each ch to end.

R2–30: Ch1. Sc in first st and each st to end. Fasten off and weave in ends.

GREY CUSHION

Front panel

Foundation chain: Ch24.

Row 1: Skip first st, sc in each st to end.

R2: Ch1. Sc in first st, *BBS into next st, sc in next st. Repeat from * to end, finishing with a sc in the final st.

R3–7: Ch1. Sc in first and each st to end.

R8: Ch1. Sc into first st, *BBS into next st, sc in next st. Repeat from * to end, finishing with a sc in the final st.

R9–11: Ch1. Sc in first and each st to end.

R12: Ch1. Sc in first st, *BBS into next st, sc in next st. Repeat from * to end, finishing with a sc in the final st.

R13–15: Ch1. Sc in first and each st to end.

R16: Ch1. Sc in first st, *BBS into next st, sc in next st. Repeat from * to end, finishing with a sc in the final st.

R17–21: Ch1. Sc in first and each st.

R22: Ch1. Sc in first st, *BBS into next st, sc in next st. *Repeat from * to end, finishing with a sc in the final st.

R23–24: Ch1. Sc in first and each st to end. Fasten off and weave in ends.

Assembling your cushions

Place the two panels together with wrong sides facing. Use a yarn needle and a length of yarn to sew around the first three sides (see page 81). Insert the cushion pad and sew up the fourth side.

Back panel

Foundation chain: Ch22.

Row 1: Skip first st, sc in each st to end.

R2–31: Ch1. Sc in first and each st to end. Fasten off and weave in ends.

Zipped pouches

Spike stitch is one of my favourite crochet stitches. Although it can be quite time consuming (as the rows don't grow very quickly), it creates a lovely thick fabric with an interesting texture. It's perfect for adding extra detail to an otherwise simple pattern such as these zip pouches. You can make the pouches in any size by changing the length of the foundation chain and the number of rows. Do note that you will need to crochet an even number of rows as the spike stitch is worked in paired rows.

YOU WILL NEED

Paintbox Simply DK yarn:
  1 × 100g (3½-oz.) ball in
  Mustard Yellow
  1 × 100g (3½-oz.) ball in
  Washed Teal
4mm hook
Scissors
Yarn needle
2 × zips: 15cm (6in) for Mustard
  pouch and 20cm (8in)
  for Teal pouch
Sewing thread to match yarn
Sewing needle

SIZES

Mustard pouch
12cm × 12cm (4¾in × 4¾in)
Teal pouch
9cm × 18cm (3½in × 7in)

SPIKE STITCH

The first row is a row of single crochet stitches. The second row is also worked in single crochet but with a slight twist – it is worked over the stitches in the first row. Instead of inserting your hook into the top of the stitch as usual, you slide it under the base of the stitch. Pull the yarn through and up in front of the stitch in a longer loop, then bring the yarn over your hook and through the two loops to complete the new stitch. Remember to ch1 at the start of each row.

Project continues overleaf

PROJECTS

MUSTARD POUCH

Foundation Row: Ch35.
Leave a 30cm (12in) tail when you make your slip knot – you'll use this to sew the seam.

Row 1–28: Work 14 paired rows of spike stitch, beginning with a row of single crochet. Fasten off leaving a 30cm (12in) tail.

<u>Assembling your pouch</u>

Fold your piece of crocheted fabric in half widthways so that the side edges lie together. Turn the pouch so that the side edges are now at the top – this will be the opening, where the zip will go. Thread the left tail through a yarn needle and sew the two sides of the left edge together (see page 81). Weave in the end of the tail (see page 78), then sew the right edge with the other tail. Use matching cotton thread and a sewing needle to stitch your 15cm (6in) zip inside the opening. Keep your stitches small and evenly spaced so they aren't visible from the outside.

TEAL POUCH

Foundation Row: Ch26.

Row 1–44: Work 22 paired rows of spike stitch, beginning with a row of single crochet. Fasten off, leaving a 30cm (12in) tail.

<u>Assembling your pouch</u>

Make up in the same way as the Mustard pouch using a 20cm (8in) zip and matching sewing thread.

Sleep masks

Although creating curved shapes such as these sleep masks may look tricky, it's actually really simple once you master how to increase and decrease (see page 58 and 59). These masks make lovely gifts, and you can even personalize them by embroidering onto the crocheted fabric.

YOU WILL NEED
Rico Essentials Cotton DK yarn:
  1 × 50g (1¾-oz.) ball in Dark Teal
  1 × 50g (1¾-oz.) ball in Dark Pink
  1 × 50g (1¾-oz.) ball in Nature
  (1 ball will make one sleep mask)
3.5mm hook
Scissors
Yarn needle

SIZE
7.5cm × 17.5cm at widest point
  (3in × 7in at widest point)

MASK (MAKE TWO)

Foundation chain: Ch9.

Row 1: Sc in second st from hook. Sc in each st to end. (8sts)
The masks are worked across from left to right in one piece, so you make one eye section, then the bit that goes across the nose and then the other eye section.

R2: Inc, sc in each of next 6sts, inc in last st. (10sts)
At the end of each row there is a number in brackets – this shows how many stitches there will be in that row once completed. The number will increase and decrease because you are adding and taking away stitches to shape the side edges.

R3: Inc, sc in each of next 8sts, inc in last st. (12sts)

R4: Inc, sc in each of next 10sts, inc in last st. (14sts)

R5–6: Sc in each st to end. (14sts)

R7: Inc, sc in each of next 12sts, inc in last st. (16sts)

R8–12: Sc in each st to end. (16sts)

R13: Dec, sc in next 14sts. (15sts)
You are decreasing on one side only, because the top edge of the sleep mask will have a flat edge and the bottom edge will be curved.

R14–15: Sc in each st. (15sts)

R16: Sc in next 13sts, dec. (14sts)

R17: Dec, sc in next 12sts. (13sts)

Project continues overleaf

PROJECTS

R18: Sc in next 11sts, dec. (12sts)

R19: Dec, sc in next 10sts. (11sts)

R20: Sc in next 9sts, dec. (10sts)

R21–25: Sc in each st to end. (10sts)
These five rows of single crochet will form the centre of the sleep mask that goes across your nose.

R26: Sc in next 9sts, inc in last st. (11sts)
Now that you are making the other side of the sleep mask, you are going to start increasing. Make sure all your increases are on the same side so you still keep a flat edge along the top.

R27: Inc in first st, sc in next 10sts. (12sts)

R28: Sc in first 11sts, inc in last st. (13sts)

R29: Inc in first st, sc in next 12sts. (14sts)

R30: Sc in next 13sts, inc in last st. (15sts)

R31–32: Sc in each st to end. (15sts)

R33: Inc in first st, sc in next 14sts. (16sts)

R34–38: Sc in each st to end. (16sts)

R39: Dec, sc in next 12sts, dec. (14sts)

R40–41: Sc in each st to end. (14sts)

R42: Dec, sc in next 10sts, dec. (12sts)

R43: Dec, sc in next 8sts, dec. (10sts)

R44: Dec, sc in next 6sts, dec. (8sts)

Fasten off and weave in the ends.

Finishing your mask

Add a slipstitch edging (see page 64) around the front of one mask – this will give it a nice neat finish. Stitch the two masks together around the outside edge using a yarn needle.

To make the strap, join your yarn to the centre of one side edge with a slipstitch and make 65 chain stitches. Check that the strap fits snugly around your head, then add or remove a few chain stitches until it does.

Join the end to the other side edge with a slipstitch, ensuring it's level with the first side. Work back along the strap with a row of single crochet stitches and slipstitch to the mask when you get to the other side. Fasten off and weave in your end.

Wall hanging

One of the many reasons I adore crochet is the incredible variety of effects you can create relatively simply. This wall hanging uses a range of stitches to make a beautifully textured boho-style piece that people won't believe has been crocheted. Although I kept mine monochrome, you could change yarn colour or add contrasting tassels.

YOU WILL NEED
Paintbox Wool Mix Super
  Chunky yarn:
  3 × 100g (3½-oz.) balls in
  Vanilla Cream
10mm hook
60cm (23in) length of wood dowel
Scissors

SIZE
35cm × 86cm (13¾in × 34in),
  including the tassels

SPECIAL STITCHES
See how to work Bobble Stitch
  (BBS) on page 112 and Spike Stitch
  on page 116.

Foundation row: Ch24.

Row 1: Skip first st, sc in each ch to end.

R2–3: Ch1. Sc in each st to end.

R4: Ch1. *Sc in next st, BBS into next st. Repeat from * to end, finishing with a sc in the last st.

R5–7: Ch1. Sc in each st to end.

R8: Ch1. *Sc in next st, BBS into next st. Repeat from * to end, finishing with a sc in the last st.

R9–10: Ch1. Sc in each st to end.

R11: Ch3. Dc in next st, *skip next st, dc in next st, ch1, dc in same st. Repeat from * to last 3sts, skip 1, dc in last 2sts.

R12: Ch3. Dc in next st, *dc in next chain space, ch1, dc in same space. Repeat from * to last 3sts, skip 1, dc in last 2 sts.

R13: *Ch4. Skip 2sts, sc into next st. Repeat from * to end, finishing with a sc in the last st.

R14: *Ch3, sc into next chain space. Repeat from * to end.

R15: *Ch2, sc into next chain space. Repeat from * to end.

R16: Sc in first st. 2sc in each chain space to end, finishing with a sc in the last st.

R17: Ch2 (counts as first st). Hdc into each stitch to end.

Project continues overleaf

PROJECTS

R18: Ch1. Sc into each stitch to end.

R19: Ch1. Work a spike stitch into each sc from the previous row.

R20: Ch1. Sc into each stitch to end.

R21: Ch1. Work a spike stitch into each sc from the previous row.

R22: Ch1. Sc into each stitch to end.

R23: Ch1. Work a spike stitch into each sc from the previous row.

R24: Ch1. Sc into each stitch to end.

R25–26: Ch4 (counts as first stitch). Tr into each stitch to end.

R27: Ch1. Sc into each stitch to end.

R28: Ch1. *Sc in next st, BBS into next st. Repeat from * to end, finishing with a sc in the last st.

R29–31: Ch1, sc into each stitch to end.

R32: Ch1. *Sc in next st, BBS into next st. Repeat from * to end, finishing with a sc in the last st.

R33–35: Ch1, sc into each stitch. Fasten off.

<u>Finishing your wall hanging</u>

Start by joining the hanging to the wooden dowel. Turn it upside down so that the first row of crochet you worked is at the top edge and the last row is at the bottom. Join the yarn to the top right corner and hold the dowel along the top edge. Work a row of single crochet around the dowel – you'll be crocheting as normal, but bring the hook up in front of the wooden dowel so the working yarn comes up behind it, enclosing the dowel within each stitch. Fasten off and weave in your ends.

Each of the 21 tassels along the bottom edge is made up of three strands of yarn, about 36cm (14in) long. Cut 63 strands of yarn, and pick out three. Fold them in half. Use your crochet hook to pull the centre loop through the first stitch along the bottom of the wall hanging and draw the loose ends through the loop. Tug to tighten, then repeat for each stitch. You can make the tassels longer if you like by cutting longer strands, or trim them all shorter when you have finished.

Plant pot covers

I'm a huge plant lover, and have quite a few plain white containers that I wanted to brighten up. Crocheted covers are the perfect way of adding a pop of colour and texture to a room, as well as livening up a boring plant pot. These are all worked in a solid colour but you could change yarns to create striped versions, use a decorative stitch instead of regular single crochet, or even adorn them with pompoms.

YOU WILL NEED
DMC Natura XL cotton yarn:
  1 × 100g (3½-oz.) ball in
  31 (cream)
  2 × 100g (3½-oz.) balls in
  41 (pink)
  2 × 100g (3½-oz.) balls in
  81 (teal)
7mm hook
Stitch marker
Scissors
Yarn needle
Plant pot(s) to cover

SIZE
Cream cover
13cm diameter at base, 16.5cm
  diameter at top, 14cm tall
  (5in diameter at base, 6½in
  diameter at top, 5½in tall)

Pink cover
9cm diameter at base, 15cm
  diameter at top, 14cm tall
  (3½in diameter at base, 6in
  diameter at top, 5½in tall)

Teal cover
14cm diameter at base, 21.5cm
  diameter at top, 17.5cm tall
  (5½in diameter at base, 8½in
  diameter at top, 7in tall)

CREAM VERSION

This pattern is for a straight-sided pot so there are no increases when working the sides, only when creating the circular base.

Round 1: Ch 4. Join with slst in first ch. 6sc into ring.
You are starting with a little ring that you will work into. Make a short row of four chain stitches, and then slipstitch into the first chain stitch, which sits next to the slip knot. You will then work six single crochet stitches, inserting your hook through the centre of the ring, not into the actual stitches.

R2: Increase in each st. (12sts)
You'll now be working in a continuous spiral, so you'll need to use a stitch marker to ensure you know when you reach the beginning of each round. Work your first single crochet of Round 2, then slip your marker underneath the top 'V' of the stitch, where you'd normally insert your hook. Crochet the rest of the round as normal.

R3: *sc in next st, increase in next st. Repeat from * around. (18sts)
You are now back to the first stitch of Round 2, where you inserted your stitch marker. Take it out and work a single crochet into the stitch. Now reinsert the marker into the top 'V' of the single crochet you've just worked. Continue crocheting as normal for the rest of this round, but remember to remove and reinsert the marker each time you start a new round.

R4: *sc in next 2sts, increase in next st. Repeat from * around (24sts)

R5: *sc in next 3sts, increase in next st. Repeat from * around. (30sts)

Project continues overleaf

PROJECTS

R6: *sc in next 4sts, increase in next st. Repeat from * around. (36sts)

R7: *sc in next 5sts, increase in next st. Repeat from * around. (42sts)
This is the last round of the flat base. Check that it is the correct size before moving on to the sides. To ensure a good fit, it should be about 1cm ($^3/_8$in) smaller all round than the base of your actual pot (as it will stretch). Add more rounds if needed, each time increasing the number of single crochets you worked before by an increase of one stitch.

R8: Sc in BLO of each st. (42sts)
You are now going to make the sides of your plant cover. The first round is worked in the back loops of the stitches only, and then the subsequent rounds will be worked as normal. This pot has straight sides, rather than being tapered, so you don't need to increase at all. Just work one single crochet in each stitch, for as many rounds as needed to get the right height. Remember to keep trying the cover on your plant pot as you go to make sure it fits properly.

R9–20: Sc in each st. Slst in first sc to join. (42sts) Fasten off and weave in ends.
Always check the round or row numbers in your pattern. Here you can see it says Rounds 9–20, which means you will work the instructions for that round for 12 rounds and not just one. When I'm crocheting multiple rounds that are all the same, I keep a tally on a scrap of paper so I know where I'm up to.

PINK VERSION

This pattern is for a smaller sized pot with tapered sides.

Round 1: Ch4. Join with slst in first ch. 6sc into ring.

R2: Increase in each st. (12sts)

R3: *sc in next st, increase in next st. Repeat from * around. (18sts)

R4: *sc in next 2sts, increase in next st. Repeat from * around (24sts)

R5: *sc in next 3sts, increase in next st. Repeat from * around (30sts)
The base of this cover has fewer rounds and stitches, as the plant pot base is smaller. Check your base size against your plant pot to ensure a good fit.

Project continues overleaf

R6: Sc in BLO of each st. (30sts)

R7–9: Sc in each st. (30sts)

So far the base has been worked in the same way as for the cream cover, but as this pot flares I had to shape the sides of the cover to fit the pot nice and snugly. After each round I popped my pot into the cover to see if it needed an increase round, so do the same with yours.

R10: *sc in next 9sts, increase in next st. Rep from * around. (33sts)

At this point my cover was getting snug on my pot so I increased slightly, by three stitches. The next few rounds I didn't need to increase as the cover still fitted the pot.

R11–13: Sc in each st. (33sts)

R14: *sc in next 3sts, increase in next st. Repeat from * around. (41sts)

The cover was getting a bit snug on the plant pot at this point, so I worked another increase round. Each time it got too tight, I added an increase round.

R15–17: Sc in each st. (41sts)

R18: * sc in next 4sts, increase in next st. Repeat from * around. (49sts)

R19–24: Sc in each st. Slst in first sc to join. (49sts) Fasten off and weave in ends.

TEAL VERSION

This pattern is for a larger sized pot with gently tapered sides.

Round 1: Ch4. Join with slst in first ch. 6sc into ring.

R2: Increase in each st. (12sts)

R3: *sc in next st, increase in next st. Repeat from * around. (18sts)

R4: *sc in next 2sts, increase in next st. Repeat from * around. (24sts)

R5: *sc in next 3sts, increase in next st. Repeat from * around. (30sts)

R6: *sc in next 4sts, increase in next st. Repeat from * around. (36sts)

R7: *sc in next 5sts, increase in next st. Repeat from * around. (42sts)

R8: *sc in next 6sts, increase in next st. Repeat from * around. (48sts)

R9: *sc in next 7sts, increase in next st. Repeat from * around. (54sts)
The base for this plant pot cover has more rounds as the plant pot is larger. You can see how each round the pattern increases by one additional single crochet stitch before every increase.

R10: Sc in BLO of each st. (54sts)

R11–17: Sc in each st. (54sts)

R18: *sc in next 8sts, inc in next st. Repeat from * around. (60sts)

R19–24: Sc in each st. (60sts)

R25: *sc in next 9sts, inc in next st. Repeat from * around. (66sts)

R26–37: Sc in each st. Slst in first sc to join. (66sts) Fasten off and weave in ends.

Storage baskets

These nifty baskets are handy for storing anything from yarn to toilet rolls and everything in between. You can easily create them in different sizes by making a few simple adjustments to the pattern. Once you've got the hang of working increases you will be able to whip up a basket in just a few hours. The cotton cord can tire your hands as it is stiffer than other yarn, so be sure to take regular breaks and stretch your fingers and wrists.

YOU WILL NEED

Bobbiny 5mm Cotton Cord:
   150m (164 yd.) in Natural
   100m (109 yd.) in Navy Blue
10mm hook
Stitch marker
Scissors

SIZES

Cream basket
30.5cm diameter × 18cm tall
   (12in diameter × 7in tall)
Navy Blue basket
24cm diameter × 14cm tall
   (9½in diameter × 5½in tall)

CREAM BASKET

Round 1: Ch4. Join with slst in first ch. 6sc into ring.
You are starting with a little ring that you will work into. Make a short row of four chain stitches, and then slipstitch into the first chain stitch, which sits next to the slip knot. You will then work six single crochet stitches, inserting your hook through the centre of the ring, not into the actual stitches.

R2: Increase in each st. (12sts)
You'll now be working in a continuous spiral, so you'll need to use a stitch marker to ensure you know when you reach the beginning of each round. Work your first single crochet of Round 2, then slip your marker underneath the top 'V' of the stitch, where you'd normally insert your hook. Crochet the rest of the round as normal.

R3: *sc in next st, increase in next st. Repeat from * around. (18sts)
You are now back to the first stitch of Round 2, where you inserted your stitch marker. Take it out and work a single crochet into the stitch. Now reinsert the marker into the top 'V' of the single crochet you've just worked. Continue crocheting as normal for the rest of this round, but remember to remove and reinsert the marker each time you start a new round.

R4: *sc in next 2sts, increase in next st. Repeat from * around. (24sts)

R5: *sc in next 3sts, increase in next st. Repeat from * around. (30sts)

R6: *sc in next 4sts, increase in next st. Repeat from * around. (36sts)

Project continues overleaf

R7: *sc in next 5sts, increase in next st. Repeat from * around. (42sts)

R8: *sc in next 6sts, increase in next st. Repeat from * around. (48sts)

R9: *sc in next 7sts, increase in next st. Repeat from * around. (54sts)

R10: *sc in next 8sts, increase in next st. Repeat from * around. (60sts)
If you would like to make a larger basket, continue with these increase rounds until the circle is the right diameter. You can create any size you like by adjusting the base, but don't forget that you'll need more yarn.

R11: Sc in BLO of each st. (60sts)
You are now going to make the sides of your basket. The first round is worked in the back loops of the stitches only and the subsequent rounds are then worked as normal, in both loops. Just work one single crochet in each stitch, for as many rounds as needed to get the right height.

R12–22: Sc in each st. (60sts)
Always check the round or row numbers in your pattern. Here you can see it says Rounds 12–22, which means you will work the instructions for that round for 11 rounds and not just one. When I'm crocheting multiple rounds that are all the same, I keep a tally on a scrap of paper so I know where I'm up to.

R23: Sc12, ch10, skip 6sts, sc24, ch10, skip 6sts, sc12.
Chaining and skipping stitches creates a gap in the crochet which will become a handle. You repeat this twice in this round so that your basket has two handles.

R24: Sc12, 14sc into space, sc24, 14sc into space, sc12. Slst in first sc to join. Fasten off and weave in ends.
For this final round, work one sc in each sc from Round 23 and 14sc into the 10 chain spaces to enlarge them.

NAVY BLUE BASKET

This pattern is for a slightly smaller basket. It's worked in exactly the same way as the larger cream basket above, but the circular base has fewer rounds.

Round 1: Ch4. Join with slst in first ch. 6sc into ring.

R2: Increase in each st. (12sts)

R3: *sc in next st, increase in next st. Repeat from * around. (18sts)

R4: *sc in next 2sts, increase in next st. Repeat from * around. (24sts)

R5: *sc in next 3sts, increase in next st. Repeat from * around. (30sts)

R6: *sc in next 4sts, increase in next st. Repeat from * around. (36sts)

R7: *sc in next 5sts, increase in next st. Repeat from * around. (42sts)

R8: *sc in next 6sts, increase in next st. Repeat from * around. (48sts)

R9: Sc in BLO of each st. (48sts)

R10–16: Sc in each st. (48sts)

R17: Sc10, ch7, skip 4sts, sc20, ch7, skip 4sts, sc10.

R18: Sc10, 9sc into space, sc20, 9sc into space, sc10. Slst into first sc to join. Fasten off and weave in ends.

Produce bags

Although these are called produce bags, they're really handy for so many things. From separating items in a baby changing bag, to popping delicates in before washing, you'll find they have plenty of uses, so make sure you crochet lots of them in different sizes. The patterns below show you how to make three variations – small, medium and large – but you can easily adapt the pattern to make any size you'd like.

YOU WILL NEED

Paintbox Cotton DK yarn:
 1 × 50g (1¾-oz.) ball each
 in Peach Orange, Blush Pink,
 Vanilla Cream, Slate Green
 or Seafoam Blue
4mm hook
Stitch marker
Scissors
Yarn needle

SIZES

Small
11cm wide × 16.5cm tall
 (4¼in wide × 6½in tall),
 unstretched

Medium
14cm wide × 23cm tall
 (5½in wide × 9in tall),
 unstretched

Large
20cm wide × 28cm tall
 (8in wide × 11in tall),
 unstretched

SMALL BAG

Foundation ring: Using Blush Pink or Seafoam Blue, make a magic ring.

Round 1: Sc6 into ring and draw up. Join with slst in first sc.

R2: *Ch2, sc into next st. Repeat from * around.
You are starting to create the net of the bag using rounds of chain stitches. Because you are working in a constant spiral, you will need to use a stitch marker, so pop it into the final single crochet you make in Round 2. Move it on each round to keep track of the number of stitches you have worked.

R3: *Ch3, sc into next chain space. Repeat from * around.
Now you are working single crochets into the spaces created by the chain stitches, rather than into the actual stitches themselves.

R4: *Ch3, sc into next chain space. Ch3, sc into same chain space. Repeat from * around.
This round is slightly different, as you are increasing the number of spaces by working two chain spaces into each chain space from the previous row.

R5: *Ch3, sc into next chain space. Repeat from * around.

R6–19: *Ch4, sc into next chain space. Repeat from * around.
The number of rounds you crochet will determine the height of your bag, so for a shorter bag crochet fewer rounds and for a taller bag crochet more rounds.

Project continues overleaf

R20: Ch1. Sc in each st around.

Rounds 20 and 21 create a solid band of crochet at the top, which helps the bag keep its shape.

R21: Ch1. *Hdc in next 4sts, ch1, skip next st. Repeat from * around. Fasten off and weave in ends.

<u>Finishing off your bag</u>

Make a drawstring by chaining 70sts. Sc into second ch from hook and each ch to end. Weave in the ends, then thread through the ch1 spaces on Round 21.

MEDIUM BAG

Foundation ring: Using Peach Orange or Slate Green, make a magic ring.

Round 1: 8sc into ring and draw up. Join with slst in first sc.

R2: *Ch2, sc into next st. Repeat from * around.

R3: *Ch3, sc into next chain space. Repeat from * around.

R4: *Ch3, sc into next chain space. Ch3, sc into same chain space. Repeat from * around.

R5–6: *Ch4, sc into next chain space. Repeat from * around.

R7–21: *Ch5, sc into next chain space. Repeat from * around.

R22: *Ch4, sc into next chain space. Repeat from * around.

R23: *Ch3, sc into next chain space. Repeat from * around.

R24: Ch1. Sc in each st around.

R25: Ch1. *Hdc in next 4sts, ch1, skip next st. Repeat from * around. Fasten off and weave in ends.

Finishing off your bag

Make a drawstring by chaining 80sts. Sc into second ch from hook and each ch to end. Weave in the ends, then thread through the ch1 spaces on Round 25.

LARGE BAG

Foundation ring: With Vanilla Cream, make a magic ring.

Round 1: 6sc into ring and draw up. Join with slst in first sc.

R2: *Ch2, sc in next st. Repeat from *around.

R3: *Ch3, sc into next chain space. Repeat from * around.

R4: *Ch3, sc into next chain space. Ch3, sc into same chain space. Repeat from * around.

R5: *Ch4, sc into next chain space. Repeat from * around.

R6: *Ch4, sc into next chain space. Ch4, sc into same chain space. Repeat from * around.

R7–27: *Ch4, sc into next chain space. Repeat from * around.

R28: *Ch3, sc into next chain space. Repeat from * around.

R29: *Ch2, sc into next chain space. Repeat from * around.

R30: Ch1. Sc in each stitch around.

R31: Ch1. *Hdc in next 5sts, ch1, skip next st. Repeat from * around. Fasten off and weave in ends.

Finishing off your bag

Make a drawstring by chaining 100sts. Sc into second ch from hook and each ch to end. Weave in the ends, then thread through the ch1 spaces on Round 31.

Market bag

This bag is made using the same technique as the produce bags, but it has a solid base to prevent small items falling out of the net, plus handles crocheted as part of the top section. For my bag I used a different colour yarn for the base, sides and top section for a colour-block effect, but you could crochet it all in one colour or just use two.

YOU WILL NEED

Rico Creative Cotton Aran:
  2 × 50g (1¾-oz.) balls in
  Light Blue
  2 × 50g (1¾-oz.) balls in
  Dark Blue
  1 × 50g (1¾-oz.) ball
  in Nature
4.5mm hook
Stitch marker
Scissors
Yarn needle

SIZE

48cm wide at top × 46cm tall
  (19in wide at top × 18in tall)

Base

Foundation ring: Using Light Blue, make a magic ring.

Round 1: 6sc into ring. Join with slst in first sc. (6sts)

R2: Inc in each st. (12sts)
You are now making the flat base from rounds of single crochet stitches. Because you are working in a constant spiral you will need to use a stitch marker, so pop it into the final single crochet you make in Round 2. Move it on each round to keep track of the number of stitches you have worked.

R3: *Sc, inc in next st. Repeat from * around. (18sts)

R4: *Sc2, inc in next st. Repeat from * around. (24sts)

R5: *Sc3, inc in next st. Repeat from * around. (30sts)

R6: *Sc4, inc in next st. Repeat from * around. (36sts)

R7: *Sc5, inc in next st. Repeat from * around. (42sts)

R8: Sc in each st around. (42sts)

R9: *Sc6, inc in next st. Repeat from * around. (48sts)

R10: *Sc7, inc in next st. Repeat from * around. (54sts)

R11: Sc in each st around. (54sts)

R12: *Sc8, inc in next st. Repeat from * around. (60sts)

Project continues overleaf

R13: *Sc9, inc in next st. Repeat from * around. (66sts)

R14: *Sc10, inc in next st. Repeat from * around. (72sts)

R15: Sc in each st around. (72sts)

R16: *Sc11, inc in next st. Repeat from * around. (78sts)

R17: Sc in each st around. (78sts)

R18: *Sc12, inc in next st. Repeat from * around. (84sts)

R19: Sc in each st around. Fasten off and weave in ends.

Sides

Join Dark Blue to any sc with a slst.

Round 1: *Ch2, skip next st, sc into next st. Repeat from * around. Insert stitch marker. Move it on each round to keep track of the number of stitches you have worked.

R2–3: *Ch3, sc into next chain space. Repeat from * around.

R4: *Ch4, sc into next chain space. Repeat from * around.

R5–25: *Ch5, sc into next chain space. Repeat from * around.

R26: *Ch4, sc into next chain space. Repeat from * around.

R27: *Ch3, sc into next chain space. Repeat from * around.

R28: *Ch2, skip next st, sc into next st. Repeat from * around. Fasten off and weave in ends.

Top section and handles

Join Nature to any sc with a slst.

Round 1: Sc in each st around. Insert stitch marker. (152sts)

R2: Hdc in each st around.

R3: *Hdc in next 5sts, ch1, skip next st. Repeat from * around.

R4: Hdc in next 33sts. Ch45, skip next 17sts, slst in next st. Hdc into same st and into next 53sts. Ch45, skip next 17sts, slst in next st. Hdc into same st and into each st around.

R5: Hdc in each st around, including chain sts. Join with slst in next st. Fasten off and weave in ends.

Finishing off your bag

Make a drawstring by chaining 200sts. Sc into second ch from hook and each ch to end. Weave in the ends, then thread through the ch1 spaces on Round 3.

Penguin toy

Amigurumi toy animals are such a fun thing to make with your new crochet skills. Don't be put off if the patterns look a bit involved – this is just because the toys are made up of a number of different small sections. Focus on one section at a time. To ease you into the world of amigurumi, this penguin toy is made up of simple shapes and worked in a chunkier yarn than the more usual DK. Once you've mastered how these basic shapes are formed, you can move on to more detailed toys.

YOU WILL NEED
Paintbox Simply Chunky yarn:
  2 × 100g (3½-oz.) balls in Slate Grey
  1 × 100g (3½-oz.) ball in Pure Black
  1 × 100g (3½-oz.) ball in Champagne White
Safety standard toy stuffing
6mm hook
Stitch marker
Scissors
Two 8mm black toy safety eyes
Yarn needle
Dressmakers' pins

SIZE
30cm (12in) tall

Head

Foundation ring: Using Champagne White, make a magic ring.

Round 1: Sc6 into ring and draw up. (6sts)

R2: Inc in each st around. (12sts)
Insert a stitch marker into the final stitch. Move it on each round to keep track of the number of stitches you have worked.

R3: *Sc, inc. Repeat from * around. (18sts)

R4: *Sc2, inc. Repeat from * around. (24sts)

R5: *Sc3, inc. Repeat from * around. (30sts)

R6: *Sc4, inc. Repeat from around. (36sts)
You have now finished your increase rounds and this is the widest point of the head section. But don't start decreasing yet, as otherwise you would end up with something that looks more like a Frisbee!

R7–12: Sc in each st around. (36sts)
The number of sc rounds, without any increases or decreases, will determine the shape of your piece. More rounds mean a longer piece, so to create a ball shape you will only work six rounds of sc.

R13: *Sc4, dec. Repeat from * around. (30sts)
Because you want the head to be the same at the top and bottom, you are now replicating what you crocheted in the increase rounds, but replacing the increases with decreases.

Project continues overleaf

PROJECTS

R14: *Sc3, dec. Repeat from * around. (24sts)

R15: *Sc2, dec. Repeat from * around. (18sts)

Insert the eyes at the centre of the head using the photograph as a guide. Stuff the head with small pieces so you don't end up with lumps. How much stuffing you put in is a matter of personal taste – some people like their toys to be firm, others like them to be more squishy. Just make sure you use enough to give your penguin structure.

R16: *Sc, dec. Repeat from * around. (12sts)

R17: Dec in each st around. Fasten off. (6sts)

When you fasten off each section, leave a long tail when you cut your yarn. You can then use these to stitch pieces together.

Body

Foundation ring: Using Slate Grey, make a magic ring.

Round 1: Sc6 into ring and draw up. (6sts)

R2: Inc in each st around. (12sts)

Insert a stitch marker. Move it on each round to keep track of the number of stitches you have worked.

R3: *Sc, inc. Repeat from * around. (18sts)

R4: *Sc2, inc. Repeat from * around. (24sts)

R5: Sc in each st. (24sts)

So far the body section has started off the same as the head, but because it will be more pear-shaped than round, you need to add some sc rounds in between your increase rounds.

R6: *Sc3, inc. Repeat from * around. (30sts)

R7: Sc in each st around. (30sts)

R8: *Sc4, inc. Repeat from * around. (36sts)

R9: *Sc5, inc. Repeat from * around. (42sts)

Project continues overleaf

R10: Sc in each st around. (42sts)

R11: *Sc6, inc. Repeat from * around. (48sts)

R12–14: Sc in each st around. (48sts)

R15: *Sc7, inc. Repeat from * around. (54sts)

R16–26: Sc in each st around. (54sts)

R27: *Sc8, inc. Repeat from * around. (60sts)

R28–32: Sc in each st around. (60sts)

R33: *Sc8, dec. Repeat from * around. (54sts)
Now you have the right body length you are going to start decreasing.
There are no sc rounds in between the decrease rounds, because the base
has to be fairly flat rather than rounded so that the penguin can sit down.
If the bottom was too rounded it would roll around.

R34: *Sc7, dec. Repeat from * around. (48sts)

R35: *Sc6, dec. Repeat from * around. (42sts)

R36: *Sc5, dec. Repeat from * around. (36sts)

R37: *Sc4, dec. Repeat from * around. (30sts)

R38: *Sc3, dec. Repeat from * around. (24sts)

R39: *Sc2, dec. Repeat from * around. (18sts)
Stuff the body, once again using small pieces of filling.

R40: *Sc, dec. Repeat from * around. (12sts)

R41: Dec in each st. Fasten off. (6sts)

Wings (make two)

Foundation ring: Using Slate Grey, make a magic ring.

Round 1: Sc6 into ring and draw up. (6sts)

R2: Inc in each st around. Insert stitch marker. (12sts)

R3: *Sc, inc. Repeat from * around. (18sts)

R4–19: Sc in each st around. (18sts)
The wing is now the right width, so now you are going to increase the length by working 15 rounds of sc.

R20: *Sc, dec. Repeat from * around. (12sts)

R21: Sc in each st around. Fasten off.

Head covering

Foundation ring: Using Pure Black, make a magic ring.

Round 1: Sc6 into ring and draw up. (6sts)

R2: Inc in each st around. (12sts)
Insert a stitch marker. Move it on each round to keep track of the number of stitches you have worked.

R3: *Sc, inc. Repeat from * around. (18sts)

R4: *Sc2, inc. Repeat from * around. (24sts)

R5: *Sc3, inc. Repeat from * around. (30sts)

R6: *Sc4, inc. Repeat from * around. (36sts)
So far you have made this the same as the head pattern, so it will fit perfectly over the crown. Now you will make the triangular point that comes down at the front of the face.

R7: Sc into each of next 8sts. Turn your work and ch1. (8sts)
From here you are just working into the 8sts from the previous row.

R8: Dec, sc4, dec. Turn your work and ch1. (6sts)

R9: Sc6. (6sts)

R10: Dec, sc2, dec. (4sts)

R11: Sc4.

R12: Dec in each st. Fasten off.

Making up your penguin

Sew the head covering to the head, matching up the centre point at the top of the head with the centre of the head covering.

Sit the bottom of the head on to the body. Use one of your yarn tails and a yarn needle to join the two together around the openings. Then use the other yarn tail to secure them two rows further out to stop the head from wobbling around.

Finally, attach your wings to the body using the yarn tails to stitch them in place. When adding limbs or wings to toys, I always recommend fixing them in place first with dressmakers' pins, so you can ensure they are positioned evenly and correctly before you stitch them down. Weave in any remaining tails. Make sure all parts of the toy are securely attached before giving it to a child.

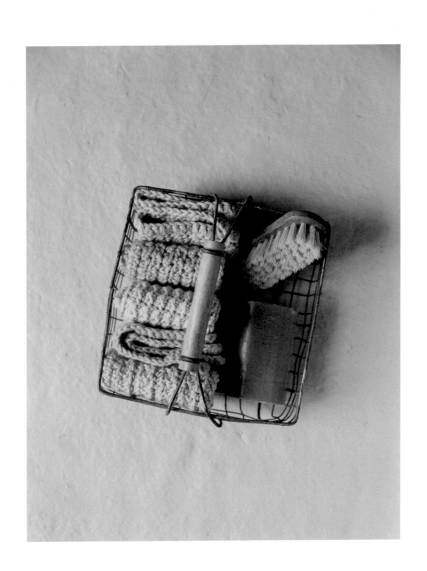

Resources

BUYING SUPPLIES

Crochet materials are becoming much more widely available – you can even find yarn in some supermarkets. But some of my favourite places to buy yarn and supplies from are:
- www.lovecrafts.com (A huge selection of brands, fast delivery and an amazing digital pattern library. They also make the amazing Paintbox yarns which are used throughout this book.)
- www.hobbycraft.co.uk
- www.thevillagehaberdashery.co.uk (A London-based store – I love to pop in and see what new yarns they have, as it's always great to see colours in real life first.)
- www.yarnplaza.com

FURTHER INSPIRATION

One of the reasons I first wanted to learn to crochet was that I followed a few online crafters who were really inspiring. Even now, I love following other crocheters, as well as chatting all things yarn. Here are a few whose work I love:

- www.twinkiechan.com
- www.martinederegtcrochetlife.blogspot.com
- www.instagram.com/yarnbae
- www.littledoolally.com
- www.instagram.com/lottieandalbert
- www.floanddot.blogspot.com
- www.mollamills.com
- www.instagram.com/annemariescrochetblog
- www.redagapeblog.com
- www.steelandstitch.blogspot.com

Crochet hashtags can also be great inspiration:

#grannysquaresrock | #amigurumilove | #kawaiicrochet | #crocheters | #crochetgirlgang | #craftastherapy | #crochetallthethings | #cornertocorner | #crochetwip | #crochetinspiration | #instacrochet | #crochetersofinstagram

About the author

Zoe Bateman is a freelance crafter, teaching craft workshops and creating craft-based projects for clients. Specializing in fibre crafts, she has had her work featured in magazines, has crocheted pieces for an art exhibition, and taught hundreds of people how to crochet.

For more on Zoe, see @toocutetoquit

Acknowledgements

This book is dedicated in loving memory to my number one, my biggest fan and cheerleader, Lou. I would not be who I am without you. Love you to the moon and back.

Hugest thank you to my Mum and Dad for your unfailing love and encouragement – this book would not have been possible without you. Thanks for listening to my ramblings, helping problem solve, giving your (often ignored!) opinions on yarn colours and just generally being amazing. And my sisters Gemma and Jadie – you've been my helpers so many times over the years, at events, packing orders, making items and generally being the best sisters in the world.

Lucy – thanks for the many cocktails, heart to hearts, and for being a 'crazy coconut.' I wouldn't have survived the last few years without you as a sounding board. Emma – my craft soulmate, thank you for always being at the other end of a frantic Instagram message and for being the only one who 'gets it'. Dee and Mary Ann, thanks for all your cheerleading and friendship, you're the best.

Thank you to all the people who have encouraged and supported me on my creative journey, giving me amazing opportunities and showing me that I could turn my love of making things into a job! Sonia and Jane for getting me into teaching workshops. Zeena for your unfailing enthusiasm, kindness, and for letting me loose making insane props. Zack for allowing me to be part of some truly amazing projects. And Gemma who showed me that you can do something you love and make it into your job.

And of course the incredible team who made this book possible. Kim for taking the most gorgeous photos and letting us take over your home. Rachel for your impeccable eye and styling. Ben for bringing it all together and turning it into an actual book (and your excellent hat-modelling skills). Studio Polka for making it look gorgeous. Lucinda and Jenny for editing it so it actually made sense to other people! And of course my commissioning editor Zena – thank you for giving me this incredible opportunity and for believing in me (and always having snacks on shoot days).

With special thanks to:

LoveCrafts and Paintbox Yarns – a massive thank you for the generous support and yarn contribution.

Lastly thank you to the creative community in general – there are thousands of people out there who have supported me over the years, from buying my products to coming to my workshops and following my journey online. Thank you for being part of this, and for allowing me to do something I truly love.

Index